God's Providence Explained

Henri Morice

God's Providence Explained

How the Lord Fashions Each Moment
and Each Event to Care for You
and Draw You Closer to Him

SOPHIA INSTITUTE PRESS®
Manchester, New Hampshire

God's Providence Explained was formerly published as *The Gospel of Divine Providence* in 1930 by the Bruce Publishing Company, Milwaukee, Wisconsin, using Rev. J. M. Lelen's translation from the French. This 1999 edition by Sophia Institute Press contains minor editorial revisions to the original text.

The cover artwork is a detail of *Flight Into Egypt* by George Hitchcock, National Museum of American Art, Smithsonian Institution, Washington, DC.

Sophia Institute Press®
Box 5284, Manchester, NH 03108
1-800-888-9344
www.sophiainstitute.com

Nihil obstat: H. B. Ries, *Censor Librorum*
Imprimatur: Samuel Stritch, Archbishop of Milwaukee
November 17, 1930

Library of Congress Cataloging-in-Publication Data

Morice, Henri, b. 1873.
    [Gospel of divine providence]
    God's providence explained : how the Lord fashions each moment
and each event to care for you and draw you closer to him / Henri Morice.
        p.   cm.
    Originally published: The gospel of divine providence. Milwaukee,
Wis. : Bruce Pub., 1930.
    ISBN 1-928832-01-6 (pbk. : alk. paper)
    1. Providence and government of God. I. Title.
BT135.M57   1999
231'.5 — dc21   99-044834

99 00 01 02 03   10 9 8 7 6 5 4 3 2 1

"What in me is dark
Illumine, what is low raise and support;
That to the height of this great argument
I may assert Eternal Providence,
And justify the ways of God to men."

John Milton
Paradise Lost

Contents

Editor's note: The biblical references in the following pages are based on the Douay-Rheims edition of the Old and New Testaments. Where applicable, biblical quotations have been cross-referenced with the differing names and numeration in the Revised Standard Version, using the following symbol: (RSV =).

God's Providence Explained

Chapter One

*You have a special place
in God's plan*

One golden evening, I paused before a bed of daisies, their petals dimmed and dusked with a tinge of amber borrowed from the western sky. As though in admiration, their faces turned toward the setting sun, with something of homage and a mute prayer in their attitude. Each of them, with its golden heart from which white petals radiated, seemed to smile to the heavens.

As I beheld them, thoughts of the relation between God and man flashed into my mind. The sun shines for us all, I mused, but we enjoy its light and heat as though we were each alone. Thus God, who excludes nothing from His solicitude, thinks of all His creatures, even the humblest. He takes particular care of each of them. A consoling thought is this, and a thought that grips us strongly if we meditate on the knowledge of God, on the way in which He communicates Himself to us, and on the plan that He has in each of His works.

God sees at once the whole and the parts

God is a king, incomparable, unique. When a human ruler issues a decree, he is far, indeed, from foreseeing all its applications. He has the general interest in view, but he cannot foresee or attend to the individual needs of all his subjects. They are too numerous; he cannot act as a father to each. Greatly gifted he may be, but his memory is short and his mind limited. If he contemplates the whole, detail escapes him, and vice versa. Examine the typography of a whole page, and you cannot distinguish one line; read a few words, and the rest is but vaguely seen by your eyes. A general who plans a campaign sees only his troops in great masses; the regiments and battalions are to him only units of combat. But when he has to examine the serviceable state, say, of one officer proposed for promotion, then he has in his mind only one individual; relegated to the dim background is the vast army.

Such is the law of the human mind. But to this law, which is caused by the poverty of our nature, the Divine Mind is not subject. There are no limitations in God. God sees with one single glance the whole and the part. Thus is answered the objection opposed to the idea of a particular Providence. Thus is answered the question: How can God busy Himself with us, since it is by laws that He governs us?

The difficulty is only apparent. To Infinite Wisdom, there is no opposition between the general and the particular. It is the same act for God to conceive a law and to think of all the cases to which it will be applied. It is by the selfsame act that He rules the universe and orients toward his destined end the child just born.

◠

God has known you from eternity
And see the beautiful consequences of this doctrine.

First, it implies the pre-existence of each one of us in the Divine Thought. We may say that during the centuries that preceded our birth, there was no question of our own little personality. As a matter of fact, at the time of Julius Caesar, no one foresaw our passage upon this earth, or our history, or our destiny.

And yet at that faraway epoch, and ages before, there was one who was interested in us. God had already set the horologe that would register the hour of our birth and had fixed our precise locus in the vastness of space. From all eternity, He has conceived all futurity. Each one of those whom He calls into existence represents one aspect of His infinite perfections. Each one of them answers a creative idea, particular and eternal. Before birth, therefore, I existed not only as a hope in the fecundity of my race, but also as an actual form in the Divine Thought.

In the depths of His eternity, God has thought of us, and among the numberless generations that are to people the earth, He has called and has chosen His own. He knows their number and their names. On the day of the final reckoning, when the just will be separated from the wicked, Christ will tell them, "Come, ye blessed of my Father, possess you the kingdom prepared for you from the foundation of the world."[1] St. Paul has said to the Ephesians, "God chose us in Him before the foundation of the world, that we should be holy and blameless in His sight in love, who predestined us to the adoption of children through Jesus Christ unto Himself."[2]

How fearful is this mystery of predestination! It is true that our salvation is absolutely in our hands, since it depends on our fidelity to divine grace. God's foreknowledge does not interfere with our liberty. Nevertheless, our destiny is settled

[1] Matt. 25:34.
[2] Cf. Eph. 1:4-5.

forever. ~~Shall I be among the saved or the lost~~? God knows the answer.

⌒

Christ knew you even during His earthly life

To redeem those whom He had chosen, God decided to send His Son into the world. Christ, who is infinite knowledge, knew each of those who were to rejoice over His coming and profit by His Sacrifice. It is their desires and their pleadings that have drawn Him down to earth. With a profound compassion, He has heard their cry of distress and has answered their appeal for the divine Messiah. "Drop down dew, ye heavens, from above; and let the clouds rain the Just One. Let the earth be opened and bud forth a Savior."[3]

Without any pride, I may, therefore, believe that I am one of the causes of the Incarnation. Infinitesimally, but positively and really, I have influenced the divine decision. And when the Word took flesh in the womb of a Virgin, He could have told me, "For thee I have done this."

During His mortal life, from experiential knowledge, Christ knew comparatively few of His countrymen and contemporaries, but in virtue of the infinite knowledge that He had as God, He knew the names of all those faithful to Him. Has He not said Himself in an exquisite allegory, "I am the Good Shepherd; and I know mine, and mine know me"?[4] He is the Shepherd of the sheep, and He calls His own sheep by name.

Now, what does He mean by these sheep? His Apostles, His disciples, His ordinary hearers? Yes. But He means also the

---

[3] Cf. Isa. 45:8.

[4] John 10:14.

Christians of all lands and all times. He alludes to them when He says, "Other sheep I have that are not of this fold; them also I must bring. And they shall hear my voice, and there shall be one fold and one Shepherd."[5]

When the divine Master preached His gospel, He had, therefore, a twofold audience: one visible and restricted; the other invisible, boundless. His eyes perceived only a group of fishermen and peasants, but beyond the limited horizon, His inward glance embraced all the faithful who, in the sequence of centuries, were to belong to Him.

We were present when Jesus taught the multitude. He has foreseen the influence that His words would have on us, and it is for us that He has uttered them. When, for instance, He represented Himself as a shepherd searching for his lost sheep, did He not think of such a sinner who today is obstinate in fleeing from Him? What an inexhaustible subject for reflection!

At times, I have envied the disciples who lived in the intimacy of the Savior, heard His voice, and felt the charm of His person. But am I not also one of the companions of Jesus? And twenty centuries before my birth, did I not occupy a place in His thought and in His heart?

In presenting to the Twelve the chalice at the Last Supper, Jesus said, "This is my blood, which shall be shed for you."[6] This formula of consecration could lead us to believe that the dying Christ had a special intention for the workers of the first hour, those who, during three years, shared His labors, His hopes, and His trials. But St. Paul tells us, with the authority of

---

[5] John 10:16.
[6] Cf. Luke 22:20.

his inspired eloquence, "He loved me and delivered Himself for me."[7] For me! Thus, the divine Crucified suffered for that ardent Pharisee who, although once a bitter persecutor, finally came to love Him so passionately.

But He did not forget us. With Pascal[8] we, too, hear Him say, "I thought of thee in my agony; there are drops of blood that I shed for thee." Oh, to think that we were there during the sorrowful agony in the lonely garden. Unseen actors in the drama of Redemption, we have contributed our share to the Passion and death of the Son of God. It is our sins that have wounded Him, nailed Him to His bed of death, and raised Him aloft upon the Cross. And when the August High Priest, both Sacrificer and Victim, offered for His executioners the first fruits of His immolation, when He cried out, "Father, forgive them, for they know not what they do,"[9] it was for all the sinners of the world — it was for you and me — that He prayed.

The character of Jesus has not changed; He is today what He was yesterday and what He ever will be.[10] In His eucharistic life, as in His suffering life, He knows all His own in general, and each one of them in particular. When we are gathered before Him, He does not see us as a confused and nameless crowd. He notices every face; His kind but searching glance penetrates each soul, even as a ray of the sun penetrates a limpid stream. The panorama of each life unrolls before Him. He

[7] Gal. 2:20.

[8] Blaise Pascal (1623-1662), French theologian.

[9] Luke 23:34.

[10] Cf. Heb. 13:8.

judges us, and His judgment is the only one that matters. Speak to Him when and how we will, therefore, and we are sure to be ever heard and understood.

Love follows knowledge. In God, neither one has any beginning. "I have loved thee with an everlasting love," He says through His prophet, "therefore have I drawn thee, taking pity on thee."[11] As He knows each of the beings He has formed, He has for each of them a particular tenderness. Indeed, true affection, which is made up of sympathy and benevolence, is addressed only to persons; to love things or collectivities of persons, we must lend them a soul; we must personify them.

☞

God's love reaches you personally

Now, do not think that because it is poured upon so many millions of creatures, divine Love loses anything of its power. What St. Thomas[12] says of the Eucharist is true also here: "Be there one, or crowds surrounding, He is equally abounding." Since His love is infinite, it can diffuse itself, without diminishing itself, over all the points of time and space. Universal, it yet remains prodigiously intense.

Does this mean that God loves infinitely each creature, and loves them all in the same manner? No. There are no two who receive the same measure of grace. Each is loved as if he were alone; his share is not deducted from that of the others.

When we study God's external manifestations, we notice the care He always takes to reach humanity in general, and

---

[11] Jer. 31:3.

[12] St. Thomas Aquinas (c. 1225-1274), Dominican philosopher and theologian.

each individual in particular. Consider the mystery of the Incarnation. When the time came foretold by the prophets, "the Word was made flesh and dwelt among us."[13] He vouchsafed to call Himself "the Son of Man,"[14] giving us the right to call Him our Brother. He made Himself our companion in exile.[15] He was reckoned in the census of mankind.[16] His manhood, however, was seen only during thirty-three years, and only within the narrow limits of Palestine. If He had not prolonged His stay upon this earth, we would have wondered why He was seen only by the Jews of His time. Such an exclusive favor would have appeared arbitrary, and scarcely worthy of Him who loves to give Himself and whose "delights are to be with the sons of men."[17]

Such a cause of dissatisfaction He has both anticipated and prevented. To all times and all places, He has extended the benefit of His Incarnation. This he has done through the Eucharist, which is His miracle of miracles, and the work of His almightiness set to serve His all-embracing love. Under the appearance of bread, Jesus is substantially present in all our churches. At any hour, we may pay Him a visit; we may worship Him and receive His regards.

True, the Apostles had an advantage on us: they saw with their eyes the incarnate Word who, since the Ascension, hides Himself beneath an impenetrable veil. But in His divine

---

[13] John 1:14.
[14] Matt. 8:20.
[15] Matt. 2:13-14.
[16] Luke 2:1-7.
[17] Cf. Prov. 8:31.

tenderness, the good Savior has made up for it. The men and women of His day could only see Him and hear Him. More favored than they, we can unite ourselves to Him and have Him as our food.

Now, one of the characteristics of our food is that it is absolutely our own. There are things possessed in common. The splendor of the sun and the perfume of flowers is everybody's property, but the mouthful of bread that I have eaten is mine and of profit only to me. And so, when I have received Holy Communion, I may say with the spouse of the Canticle of Canticles, "My Beloved to me, and I to Him."[18] In the heart-to-heart thanksgiving, He is mine, wholly mine.

How truthful was St. John when he cried out, "Having loved His own who were in the world, He loved them unto the end."[19] "Unto the end": that is to say, to the greatest extreme, to an excess, to a paroxysm of love — to a folly of love. In the Upper Room, Christ finishes the work begun at Nazareth. There He gave Himself to humanity; here He gives Himself to each one of us.

The same remark can be made concerning the mystery of redemption. On Calvary, the Son of God offered Himself once for all. Unceasingly on the altar, He renews this Sacrifice and applies the fruits thereof to all mankind. Endowed with the magnanimity of Christ, the Church commands her priests to pray for all the faithful, living or dead. Each of the hundreds of thousands of Masses said every day brings grace, therefore, to all Christians. Yet the distribution of this grace is not uniform.

---

[18] Cant. 2:16 (RSV = Song of Sol. 2:16).
[19] John 13:1.

The whole resolves itself into many wholes. Some receive a more abundant effusion of grace than others: the priest who celebrates, those who attend the Mass and thus cooperate with him in the holy action, and especially those for whom the sacrifice is offered at their request. Twice such specification is made. The priest remembers the living before the Consecration, but through an exquisite rule and rubric, he waits for Jesus to be on the altar to speak to Him of the dead. Thus, thanks to the Mass, which renews it, the merits of the sacrifice are distributed and placed, as it were, into our own hands.

Such dispensation has its complement in the sacraments, which have been instituted for all men in general and for each man in particular. They are means of individual sanctification. Each one of us must personally go to them and prepare himself to receive them. Seldom are Baptism and Penance administered collectively. Except in such case of necessity, people are baptized, absolved, and confirmed individually. The sacraments are, therefore, channels that bring to each man individually a parcel of grace merited by Christ. If I may use a homely comparison, they are like the system of conductors that convey and distribute into our homes the water kept in a general reservoir.

God fills the world with variety

God, who gives Himself to each of His own, has also a special design for each of them. The world in which I live is a combination of forces and of laws, of individuals and of events. Either with the same elements or with a different material, an infinity of other combinations would be possible. God, who is wisdom itself, has chosen the one that would bring Him greatest glory. When He chose this one, He knew how it would operate; He knew all its pieces and movements.

Now, I am one wheel of that great machine, an intimate wheel, which has its place and plays its part. God had me in view when He created things. I am one of the reasons He selected this universe in preference to others.

But what does God expect of me? What is the particular function I must fulfill? If I place myself on a natural plane, I see only this: that I must enhance the beauty of the world. The Creator delights in His work. He knows and admires it and would draw glory from it even if no creature were able to praise Him. This is why the psalmist tells us that the heavens proclaim the glory of God.[20]

Now, not only its grandeur and unity, but also its variety, contribute to the beauty of the universe. It seems that God has taken pleasure in multiplying indefinitely all the forms of life. On our globe, "on this little O, the earth," we can count hundreds of thousands of plant and animal species. In each species, there are varieties, and in any of these varieties, one would seek vainly for two identical individuals. Each has its proper characters; each reflects the divine splendor in its own way. Imperceptible as it may be, it therefore adds to the beauty of the world.

"If you would know how much the world will miss you when you are dead, put one of your thumbs into a tub of water, then pull it out and look for the hole you have dug," said an American humorist, and there is truth in his saying. We are indeed very little. No one can flatter himself by thinking that

[20] Ps. 18:2 (RSV = Ps. 19:1).

he is indispensable. There is no man who cannot be spared. Life in the forest is not interrupted because one flower has faded away. And yet, if it had not smiled even for only a day, the woodland would have been not quite so beautiful. A note would have been missing from the universal harmony if you or I had not sung our song.

$\approx$

You have a particular role in God's plan

Now, if we examine the problem from a supernatural viewpoint, we understand more clearly why each of us has a special vocation.

The society of the faithful is a temple of which Christ is the Architect. In this edifice, vast as the world, there are stones that are conspicuous and others that are hidden; some are chiseled with care; others are scarcely chipped off. But, little or great, rough or adorned, whatever its form and place, each has its own reason for being there. In that artistic construction, where everything is foreseen to the least detail, nothing is missing; nothing is in excess.

See, for instance, the saints who have been canonized. Imitators of Christ, they labored all their lives to conform themselves to the divine Model. Must we, then, conclude that they all resemble one another? No, indeed. All saints are originals. Each makes his own contribution to the common character of Christian spirituality.

A similar observation can be made concerning religious orders. The members of a congregation are trained according to the same method, often in the same novitiate, and by the same teachers. Does this mean that they are cast in the same mold, done in series, and interchangeable? No. The nature is corrected, made as perfect as possible, but not destroyed. And as water shapes itself according to the outlines of its container, so the spirit of a congregation is formed according to the personalities of the individuals therein. They all have common principles, the same family appearance, but under the uniformity of garb and manner, the personal character ever appears.

The fact that keeping the rule of an institution leaves one's personality intact is strikingly proved by the case of St. Thérèse of Lisieux.[21] She entered Carmel at an age when character was not finally formed. No nun was more docile, submissive, and God-trusting. Therefore, it seems as if her individuality would have dissolved itself in the common life, as a flake of snow in a stream. Far from being commonplace, however, Thérèse of the Child Jesus had her own character, her own spirit, and her own striking individuality. According to her own manner, she conceived an ideal of Christian perfection and marched toward it along her own little path. She would love God as a small child loves her father, with humility, confidence, and self-surrender.

She did not go so far as to deny the favors she had received; that would be voluntary blindness and ingratitude. But she knew her imperfections and her weakness. When she compared herself to the giants of sanctity, she saw herself as a grain of dust beside a mountain. But precisely because she was small and feeble, she confided in God, who proportions His graces to our needs. She did not doubt His mercy. When a baby stumbles, he does not fall from a great height, and Thérèse never committed any grave fault, but if she had stained her white

[21] St. Thérèse of Lisieux (1873-1897), Carmelite nun.

soul with the blackest of sins, she would have rushed into the arms of her eternal Father, sure to obtain pardon. The child who dies before the age of reason is not condemned to Hell; so it does not seem that the possibility of her being a castaway has ever troubled the mind of Thérèse. A lively sentiment of divine goodness filled her with hope and joy. She abandoned herself to God's Providence as a baby who glides into caressing arms.

Now, to love God as a child loves a father, and to find in such unique disposition humility, confidence, self-surrender, and peace — this is what Thérèse calls her "little way." According to her, no way is more direct nor rapid. Others rise to perfection on stairs that can be ascended only step by step. "I," she says, "straightway go up on an elevator."

Have we also a special vocation? Certainly, and we would know how to discover it if we had the spirit of prayer. God has His special plan for each one of us. A comforting truth this is, especially for persons who think themselves useless. Not finding any immediate task at hand, being ignored, perhaps, in the sphere in which they are placed, they sometimes say to themselves, "What am I doing upon this earth? God has created me in vain." This is not true, for God never creates anything without a design. We must make use of His gifts.

But His aim is not always so glorious as we may have fondly expected. Instead of placing us upon the candlestick, He hides us under the bushel. What He asks us is, for instance, to rear an orphan, to assist aged parents, to care for a sick brother, or, still more simply, to give the example of resignation in trials and of dignity in the midst of destitution. Such tasks are as many as there are individuals. In the hive of the Church, each bee must construct its own cell and distill its own drop of honey.

In view of this special distinction, God distributes the natural and supernatural gifts, and combines and correlates the events of our life. He selects the place and the date of our birth; He contrives the influence of heredity and education. These are as tiny strokes that fashion, little by little, our body and our soul. He prepares us for the service that we must render; He adapts us to our specialty. If, out of pure whim or by mistake, we take a wrong direction, He stops us, and as soon as we set foot on the right road, obstacles disappear. His discreet interventions determine the orientation of our life even more than the choice of our will does.

Unbelievers claim that such things are sheer conjectures, chimeras of vain souls who believe themselves interesting enough to be seen by the eyes of God. Let them say what they will; our faith in a special Providence rests on solid ground — the very word of God. To prove this assertion, let me quote a passage from the Bible.

In the book of Isaiah, God tells us through His prophet that, having decided to make Cyrus the deliverer of His people, He designated him by name and prepared his ways. "Thus saith the Lord to my anointed Cyrus, whose right hand I have taken hold of, to subdue nations before his face, and to turn the backs of kings, and to open the doors before him, and the doors shall not be shut. I will go before thee and will humble the great ones of the earth. I will break in pieces the gates of brass and will cut asunder the bars of iron, and I will give thee the hidden treasures and the concealed riches of secret places, that thou mayest know that I am the Lord who call thee by thy name, the God of Israel. For the sake of my servant Jacob and Israel my chosen, I have even called thee by thy name; I have surnamed thee though thou hast not known me. I am the Lord, and there is none else; there is no God besides me. . . . I made the earth, and I created man upon it. My hand stretched forth the heavens, and I have commanded all their host. I have raised him up to justice, and I will direct all his ways. He shall build my city and let go my captives, not for ransom, nor for presents, saith the Lord, the God of hosts."[22]

So, according to Holy Spirit, God entrusts Cyrus with a special mission for which He Himself prepares him and of which He favors the fulfillment.

Now, because it is true that God has a special end for each one of us, He will examine us at the term of our life about the manner in which we have served His design. We shall all appear at the same moment in the great gathering at the General Judgment, but a long time before that, our destiny shall be decided. God does not judge men in the mass. He studies the case of each one and carefully weighs his works, good or bad. On the very spot of death, a veil is lifted, and straightway the soul stands before God, who is everywhere. The Supreme Judge looks at the soul and demands an account of its stewardship. Blessed are we if we may answer like Him who was sent to save the world: "I have finished the work which Thou gavest me to do."[23]

⌒

The Father is both God of all and God of each

In ethical and religious questions, error oftentimes covers truth, like the slag that hides and tarnishes the nuggets of gold.

[22] Isa. 45:1-13.
[23] John 17:4.

You have a special place in God's plan

The ancient people of Latium thought that each tribe had as its exclusive property, a particular god, a tutelary genius. Far from recruiting worshipers to such a god, they jealously hid his name; hidden also were the traditional rites celebrated in his honor and the magical formulas by which his intervention was obtained. Proselytism was then absolutely unknown. Alone the new bride was initiated to the family cult, and only on condition that first she would abjure the gods of her ancestors. For the first Latins then, religion was a sort of pact concluded between a tribe and a divinity. The tribe pledged itself to honor only its god, and, in return, the god had to protect it to the exclusion of all others.

Verily, no belief could be more contrary to the spirit of the gospel. To us, the heavenly Father whom Jesus has revealed is not the God of the Jews, nor is He the God only of mankind. He is the Creator, the sovereign Master of the universe, and there is none other beside Him. Every intellect must adore Him; every knee must bow before Him in Heaven and on earth. For His own part, He embraces His whole work and despises none of His creatures.

Thus, Christianity satisfies human reason, which, although ever so little enlightened, acknowledges God's unity. But it also answers our need to be personally known, loved, and protected. If God were merely a faraway monarch, wisely administrating His immense kingdom, but having no regard for our sufferings and prayers, how cold would be our piety! Lost in the wilderness of creatures, we would feel like orphans. The wisest laws are not worth a single wave of fatherly tenderness.

But as we have seen, God is not an administrator who considers things from on high and takes no interest in the general march of our affairs. He ignores and neglects none of His children. We call Him "our Father" to acknowledge our common filiation, but when we consider Him as our benefactor, when, amid dangers of soul and body, we make an appeal to His goodness, we cry out, "My God!" At times we even say, "My Jesus!" for, although the Word has been incarnate for all men, to each one of us He gives Himself in Holy Communion. Profoundly true is this utterance of His to the saint of Avila:[24] "Thou art Teresa of Jesus, and I am Jesus of Teresa."

God's angels and saints protect and assist you

This particular characteristic of the universal religion is strikingly exhibited in the devotion to the guardian angels and to holy patrons.

According to Holy Scripture, the functions of the angels may be reduced to three: they execute God's will, they carry messages, and they protect men. The three illustrious archangels — Michael, Gabriel, and Raphael — represent each of these missions. It was Michael who led the heavenly army against the rebel Satan;[25] Gabriel was entrusted with the glorious message of the Incarnation;[26] and Raphael conducted the young Tobias on his journey and brought him back home.[27] We see in the Gospel that Jesus Himself was served, defended, and consoled by angels.[28] He tells us of those heavenly spirits

---

[24] St. Teresa of Avila (1515-1582), Carmelite nun and mystic.

[25] Apoc. 12:7-9 (RSV = Rev. 12:7-9).

[26] Luke 1:26 ff.

[27] Tob. 5 ff.

[28] Cf. Matt. 4:11; Luke 22:43.

who, while seeing the little ones entrusted to them, see also the face of His Father who is in Heaven.[29] In the book of Revelation, mention is made of angels, protectors of Churches.[30] And we read in the Acts of Martyrs this word of St. Cecilia[31] to Valerianus: "There is a secret which I wish to tell thee: I have an angel of God who loves me, and with great jealousy guards my body."

It seems strange that, to avert dangers from us or to communicate His graces to us, God uses intermediaries. Could He not come directly? No doubt. But to realize His designs, it pleases Him to make use of His creatures. By such means, He obtains a twofold advantage: He helps us and gives to the angels the occasion to imitate His mercy. They cannot assist each other, since they are perfectly happy, but their goodness exercises itself over their inferior brethren, even as, in large families, the older take care of the younger and pour on them something of the tenderness that they have received.

Although the angels are incomparably superior in knowledge, in power, and in sanctity, we are their brethren. We have the same origin, the same love, and the same destiny. Their aim and our aim are the same; they possess what we hope for. So they watch over us with tender solicitude. Discreet and unselfish, they follow us step by step, and when the invisible world that surrounds ours is revealed, we shall be amazed by all the services that they have rendered us.

---

[29] Matt. 18:10.

[30] Cf. Apoc. 2:1 (RSV = Rev. 2:1).

[31] St. Cecilia, second- or third-century martyr and patron saint of musicians.

Guardian angels are given to us also to counteract the influence of the demons. Enraged against God and jealous of men, Satan does all he can to lead us into perdition. Through him, the temporal goods that tempt us flash before our eyes. It is he who says, "All these will I give Thee, if, falling down, Thou wilt adore me."[32]

Since the wicked spirits try to seduce us, why should not the good angels strive to maintain us in grace with God? To baffle the wiles of the tempter and to guard us against his snares are their principal tasks. So, between the powers of Heaven and those of Hell, a desperate fight is fought, and we are the stake. Our duty is to offer our hand to our celestial friend and to contribute to a victory in which we are so interested.

Again, it is a pious belief that the saints especially protect those faithful who are called by their name and the communities placed under their patronage. Christians' attachment to a patron saint arises not only from their confidence in his power and admiration for his virtues, but also from gratitude for his benefits and perhaps the remembrance of some distant kinship. He is their appointed protector; he is their ambassador with God. In all their difficulties, it is to him that they preferably go.

And one easily understands that uprooted Celt who sadly said, "The saints of my new country do not understand me here." He forgot that the city of God is without limits. Nowhere is a Christian a stranger to the land. Whithersoever he goes, his prayer is heard. So let us see in that simple plaint only

[32] Matt. 4:9.

the expression of a sentiment as old as mankind that Christianity, appropriating to itself what is best in ancient religions, has adequately satisfied: the need of a special protection.

We Catholics know that Christ has promised infallibility not to the sheep but to the shepherds to whom He has given the mandate to teach. To them He has said, "He that heareth you, heareth me; and he that despiseth you, despiseth me. And he that despiseth me, despiseth Him that sent me."[33] Hence, it follows that an opinion contrary to the teaching of the Church comes not from God, but from deceitful powers. Christ does not recognize as His own those who will not obey His representatives.

God speaks to you personally

But within the limits of dogma, there remains much room for personal inspiration. Many saints have had visions and particular revelations. God speaks to us in the intimacy of our conscience. Remorse, yearnings for a better life, call to apostleship or priesthood: all these are divine inspirations. If we were less fascinated by the things of the senses and more attentive to our interior life, we would see that not one day passes when we do not receive from on high some warning or some appeal.

Let it not be said that our piety is all exterior formalism and that we observe uncritically the same rubrics and unconvincingly repeat the same ritualistic formulas. The truth is that each one of us has personal relations with God. Every hour and in all manners, His grace solicits us. Sometimes we yield

[33] Luke 10:16.

to His commands, and sometimes we resist them; hence, an interior drama whose action varies with each individual. In pious souls, habitually recollected, the spiritual life is still more profound and more variegated, and, because it runs into a channel, its course is more peaceful and limpid.

☙

God provides for each of His creatures

For some time, as we read in his *Apologia*, John Henry Newman's motto was "Myself and my Creator!" What does this mean exactly? Does it mean that the soul, dazzled by divine splendors, ignores created things? But then it would forget itself and not speak of its "ego." What, then, is Newman's thought? Is he so taken up with the labor that grace operates in him that he is totally absorbed by such a view? But he is not the only theater of divine operations. What God's Providence has done for him it has done for many others, and it is especially in this that it is admirable.

One understands that a mother who has three or four children interests herself in each of them and keeps acquainted with the life incidents of each one. But God's Providence watches over millions and millions of creatures and provides for the needs of each of them. Who would not admire such a universal and minute solicitude? During the Great War, it was a very complex problem to ration the troops and to distribute to each soldier bread to feed himself and munitions to defend himself. But what is such a problem compared with the problem that God's Providence solves every day?

Numberless eyes dulled by suffering or brilliant with hope turn toward Him, and, wise as well as good, He ministers to the needs of each. "He openeth His hand and filleth with blessing every living creature."[34] Not only does He preserve the physical life, but He also feeds and fortifies the soul. He directs each free will toward its end, and for that purpose, He invents combinations of graces and of events that are as wonderful, in a sense, as the general economy of Redemption. Each one is worth what it has cost, and it may be said that our soul is as precious as the whole world.

And yet we would not accept without reserve Newman's formula: "Myself and my Creator!" If we look upon ourselves merely from an individual standpoint, the more wondrous side of the divine work escapes us. But without forgetting that we have myriads of brethren, it is lawful to think with greater gratitude of the particular care of which we are the object.

O God's Providence, when I consider the
numberless number of creatures which Thou protectest,
I am terrified by Thy power. But when I re-enter into myself
and remark with what perseverance, what attentions, and what
delicacy Thou followest my path of life, I am both touched and
amazed. I have a glimpse of Thy grandeur; I feel how unique
Thou art, for who can give himself to one and to all?
Each one has his share, and all have it entire.
Only the Infinite can thus be communicated.
And so I am loved by Thee as though I were alone.
How proud would I be of such a favor
were I less unworthy of it!

[34] Ps. 144:16 (RSV = Ps. 145:16).

Chapter Two

Providence enlightens, consoles, and draws you to God

If, during its flight from the muzzle to the target, a projectile could be aware of the trajectory it describes, it would believe itself master of its motion; and yet it merely follows the impulsion given by the marksman.

So it is with us. How many men, jealous of their independence and impatient of any yoke, believe themselves to be the arbiters of their destiny! They accept no guide but their reason and no spur but their desires. If they remain obstinately deaf to the promptings of grace, God, by and by, abandons them to the leaders they have chosen, and they thus become castaways.

As to docile souls, He leads them with exquisite delicacy, and, without restricting their liberty, makes them serve His designs. His eyes are fixed on them all at the same time, and He cares for each of these souls as if it were alone.

By what means does God direct souls toward the end assigned by Him?

Such means are twofold: interior and exterior. God enlightens our mind, touches our heart, and strengthens our will. For the good of those faithful to Him, He uses also events and men and, in general, all His creatures. We shall, then, first consider His workings on our soul; afterward, we shall see the instruments that He uses.

God's Providence Explained

God enlightens your mind

St. John tells us that Christ is "the true Light which enlighteneth every man that cometh into this world."[35] Hence, it follows that the Word is the reason of all things, the luminous focus of which our intellect is a reflection, the book that, often unconsciously, is consulted by all minds.

Everywhere present, and speaking all languages, He also gives, if one may say so, private lessons to each of His disciples. He teaches them without words, either in giving them new ideas, or in renewing the impression of truths they already know.

It is an article of Faith that the inspired authors wrote under the inspiration of God. Each of our sacred books could begin with the formula used by the prophets: "Thus says the Lord."[36] Our Lord Himself came as the messenger of the heavenly Father and the herald of the great King: "My doctrine is not mine, but His that sent me."[37]

The book of Revelation is the last of the inspired books. Having taught by His prophets and by His Son all the truths necessary to salvation, God will make no more revelations. Does this mean that communications between Heaven and earth have ceased? No. God will no more address any biblical message to mankind, but He will not cease instructing human souls. He is the Truth who speaks inwardly and manifests Himself silently.

[35] John 1:9.
[36] Exod. 4:22.
[37] Cf. John 14:24.

Some experience God in mystical ways

In studying the life of great mystics, one is astonished at the place occupied by apparitions, visions, revelations, and prophecies. There exists a world that is near ours; an opaque veil separates us from it — so much so, that many never think of it, or at least pay no great attention to it. But to mystics, the curtain is lifted at intervals, disclosing radiant perspectives.

Hence the singular charm of St. Teresa's writings. If it is true that poetry is a faint gleam of ideal beauty, what is more beautiful than her confidences? From the lofty lodges of the soul's castle, she perceives horizons incomparably more vast and beautiful than ours. The hereafter, which to us seems so far away, so mysterious, is to her a vivid reality, close to her. Supernatural splendors illumine her mind. More than once, she had knowledge of future events that could not have been foreseen by human means.

Often, also, a heavenly gleam illuminating her intellect led her to understand the truths of Faith. In a short space of time spent in prayer, she would receive more light than we, with our earthly studies, could acquire in years. She would see herself suddenly enriched with priceless treasures, without knowing how she acquired them. Truth entered into her, as Jesus entered through the closed doors into the room where His Apostles prayed.[38]

In the last chapters of her autobiography, St. Teresa narrates the visions that were lavished upon her. One day, without any warning of such a favor, she felt our Lord near her, on

---

[38] John 20:19.

her right side. So clear and so lifelike was the feeling of the divine presence that she became frightened. Later, months later, He appeared to her, as He did on Mount Tabor, in a dazzling light.[39] Seeing Him, St. Teresa understood why the devils tremble before the majesty of Almighty God. But she, the spouse of Christ, now did not tremble. Her heart overflowed with gratitude, and, every day, her charity became more ardent.

God speaks to some in dreams

Such visions and revelations are the privilege of the few. But are those whom grace does not call into the mystical ways completely deprived of all communications with Heaven? Does not God speak to some in dreams?

It is dangerous treading here, as Francis Thompson would say, yet with reverence I venture. Wisdom advises us, in keeping with the Holy Scriptures, not to attach great importance to dreams. What are they usually but a series of incoherent images, the simple mental rendering of a physiological state? All their elements are borrowed from our previous life, so much so, that they have been described as only the events of yesterday produced anew by a fatigued brain. Shakespeare calls them:

> The children of an idle brain
> Beget of nothing but vain fantasy,
> Which is as thin of substance as the air
> And more inconstant than the wind.[40]

[39] Matt. 17:1-2.
[40] William Shakespeare, *Romeo and Juliet*, Act 1, scene 4.

There are, however, dreams that come from Heaven — for instance, that of the wise men from the East,[41] that of St. Joseph,[42] and many others mentioned in the Bible. We read in the book of Job: "God speaketh once, and repeateth not the selfsame thing the second time; by a dream in a vision by night, when deep sleep falleth upon men, and they are sleeping in their beds; then He openeth the ears of men and . . . instructeth them in what they are to learn."[43] It is, then, lawful and reasonable to believe that God may speak to the soul through dreams, for the influence of God extends to sleeping as well as to waking hours. Such occurrences, however, are rare, and we have mentioned the subject merely because of its possibility.

⌒

God speaks to your conscience

But now we are on safer ground, and we say that God enlightens us in the midst of spiritual and physical dangers.

When temptation urges us to sin, He speaks to us through the still, small voice of conscience and unceasingly tells us, "Do not do this." This voice, although less clamorous than that of passion, is still very clear and commanding. If we lend our ear to it, it becomes stronger and draws us to do good. But if, by languor or lassitude, by weakness or malice, our attention gives way, the voice is as if stilled in the clamor of a raging tempest.

After we commit a sin, the voice is heard anew. Passion once stifled now hears duty's voice. How vehement the first

---

[41] Matt. 2:12.

[42] Matt. 1:20, 2:13.

[43] Job 33:14-16.

remorse! How solemn the warnings of conscience! How indignant it is against sin and against scandal! Woe to those who destroy the temple of God! Woe to the workers who are destroyers instead of builders!

⌒

God speaks to you through inspiration

In an unforeseen danger, sometimes without any calculation or reflection, we do the very best thing to avoid it. It is as though a superior intellect, supplanting our hesitant and frantic mind, directs our person.

One day, as I was crossing a street, an automobile that I had not seen nor heard, bore down upon me at full speed. By a sudden inspiration, I stopped, and the machine just grazed me without hurting me. I recognized afterward that I had done instinctively the very best thing I could have done. To take a step forward or backward would have been a false move. But as I remained motionless, the driver, who could see better than I did, veered his machine and avoided me.

Whence come such inspirations that occur so frequently? From the instinct of self-preservation, say certain thinkers; they are irruptions from the subliminal consciousness to the clear consciousness. But are they not rather suggestions from the good Providence of God, who sees all our steps and guards us in all our ways?

To see the road we must follow is not enough. To know the truth is not the same as to feel it and live it. Some of our thoughts are active; others seem dead and have no appreciable influence over our conduct. We know, for instance, that the hour of our death is uncertain, but has this truth entered into the substance of our soul? If we felt the frailty of all things, if we were convinced that, at any moment, our being can be dissolved as a flake of snow touched by a flame, this would be enough to change the trend of our lives.

God, who thoroughly knows our nature and the secret springs that move it, takes care to renew and refresh our ideas so that they become more active. To lead us wherever He wills, He has no need to resort to revelations. In Christian countries, nearly all people know the essential truths. God merely sets them off, projects over them His light, and thus gives them the brightness and drawing force of a revelation.

It is especially in meditation that such inspirations occur. To meditate is to draw our ideas from the shadows and place them before our inward vision. Our thoughts are usually buried in the depths of our soul; meditation unfolds and displays them. It does not, however, complete our task. Our intellect stirs the ideas and expresses them, but it happens that God mingles His voice with our word; among the humble weavings of our reflections, He inserts, as golden threads, supernatural inspirations. Although discreet and veiled, His action is nonetheless efficacious. During the course of meditation, we are sometimes visited with unexpected thoughts that excite within us a flame of enthusiasm. Let us welcome with joy these heavenly messengers, and let them carry us Heavenward.

⁀

God speaks to you through sermons

To refresh our ideas, God also uses the sermons we hear. It is a well-known fact that a child learns better from a teacher than from a book. Why such a difference? Is the instructor's lesson more complete or more clear? No, for there are handbooks that leave nothing to be desired from the standpoint of precision or clearness. But the fact is that the book is only blackened paper; it is dead. The teacher is a living soul, and because he understands, he can make others understand.

On the wings of the spoken word, truth flies from one intellect to another. Likewise, when a speaker is saturated with his subject, when he feels fervently what he says, his fervor is contagious. He holds and uplifts his audience. In him everything speaks: the attitude, the look, the gesture, and especially the expressive accent, "that sound from the heart which reaches the heart."

Let not the sowers of words, however, take pride in their success. It is not their eloquence that makes converts, but, rather, God's grace given by Him on such occasions.

During missions and retreats, priests are sometimes witnesses of consoling returns to God. A person comes and says, "Father, your sermon has touched me. I will give up my sinful life." And when the priest, curious to understand this work of grace, asks the convert what has moved him in his instruction, he finds with surprise that it was not the strength of his arguments nor the vehemence of his speech. Usually it was an afterthought, a commonplace phrase uttered incidentally. But of such a slight thing God has made great use: He has made it an instrument in opening the fissure through which grace has entered a soul.

At other times there are circumstances that serve to shed light upon the soul. Truth is displayed under a new and more striking aspect; and when such events are tragic, they move the soul to its very depths and rid it of all prejudice, even as those squalls which, stirring the sands of a wilderness, reveal the monuments buried beneath.

God speaks through Scripture

One day, a man who for years had abandoned all religious practices entered a church during High Mass. He came not for the purpose of honoring God, but only to obtain shelter during a storm. The pastor went to the pulpit. He was an old man, tall and ascetic-looking. Slowly, gravely, he uttered the words: "Come to me, all you that labor and are burdened, and I will refresh you."[44] The visitor knew quite well that sentence of the Gospel, but never had it struck him as it did at that moment. He saw in a flash the infinite goodness of God, which strives to save sinners stubbornly rushing to perdition. Moved by grace, he resolved to change and became a fervent Christian.

Still more moving are the circumstances of the conversion of Count Schouvaloff. Broken by sorrow, he was reading the Gospel of St. John at the deathbed of his wife. The ardent desire to remain united to her whom he had deeply loved made him find delight in the words of Jesus: "That they all may be one, as Thou, Father, in me, and I in Thee; that they also may be one in us."[45] He understood that, in spite of appearances, the dead are not separated from the living, but form with them one selfsame spiritual city, or, rather, one body animated by Christ. He understood that the separation of churches is contrary to the divine will: "And other sheep I have that are not of this fold: them also I must bring. And they shall hear my voice, and there shall be one fold and one Shepherd."[46] Count

---

[44] Matt. 11:28.
[45] John 17:21.
[46] John 10:16.

Schouvaloff, solemnly weighing these words, saw all their bearings. The light of God dispelled his prejudices against Rome, and abjuring the schism, he became a Catholic.

☞

God conceals things that it
would harm you to know

Every truth is not good to know. We must not be surprised that sometimes, instead of enlightening our mind, God hides what our mind must not see.

There is, for instance, in some saints a humility that seems excessive. Everybody admires them, but they despise themselves. In spite of their mortification, zeal, and piety, they think they are great sinners, unworthy of divine mercy. In spite of all the good they do, they believe themselves to be useless servants. As a fruitful vine, they bear fruit unconsciously. You say it is an illusion. Very well, but it is a beneficent illusion. God allows it to preserve them from vain complacency, which would be for them the most dangerous of temptations.

For the same reason, He leaves us in uncertainty concerning our eternal future. What will be our destiny beyond the grave? Shall we hear the divine Word: "Come, ye blessed of my Father, possess you the kingdom prepared for you from the foundation of the world"?[47] Who can say? This is why St. Paul advises us to work out our salvation in fear and trembling.[48] "I am not conscious to myself of anything. Yet am I not hereby justified, but He that judgeth me is the Lord,"[49] he tells us.

---

[47] Matt. 25:34.
[48] Phil. 2:12.
[49] 1 Cor. 4:4.

Every day, we ask God that we may not be led into temptation. He grants this prayer, not only in removing from us the occasions of sin, but in preventing us from seeing such occasions. Because of their inborn candor, many young men full of good will, but of weak character, have resisted the siren's advances and temptations. They have not understood her innuendoes. Their ignorance or their timidity has preserved them from downfall and sin.

Natural modesty plays in the moral order the same role that eyelids play in the physical order. Eyelids go down as soon as dazzling brightness menaces the vision; so modesty guards against too-strong emotions and against premature revelations. It is a mark of innocence and one of its best safeguards.

⌒

God gently draws you to Him

If our nature were perfectly controlled, there would be always a proportion between our desires and their object; and since God is "so good that none can be better," it is He who would then have the best place in our heart. In fact, we aspire toward Him; He is the center toward which all the superior tendencies of our soul converge. But we are so deeply plunged into the material that almost anything deflects and disturbs movement toward the supreme God, even as the least electrical current moves and maddens the magnetic needle which no more looks on the magnetic pole.

How will our nature, disorganized by Original Sin, find again its equilibrium? How will what is most lovable become the most loved? This can be done only with the help of God's grace. The holy desires it excites within us counterbalance the carnal desires and tear us from the seduction of creatures.

This is the reason God moves our heart and enlightens our mind at the same time. He intervenes in the life of our heart in provoking attractions or repulsions, and in alternating His consolations and trials. The soul, being naturally Christian, feels a general attraction for God, whom it seeks, sometimes unconsciously, under the names of love, perfection, and bliss. But grace inspires also within us particular attractions for such and such a kind of life, such and such a virtue, or such and such an undertaking.

Christ said in speaking of Himself, "Behold, a greater than Solomon is here."[50] Indeed, what was the material Temple built by the heir of David compared with the spiritual temple that is being built by the Son of God? This splendid edifice will be finished only at the end of time. Like laborers who work continuously, shift after shift, generations are working at it, every one in its turn.

The divine Architect selects His workers one by one and assigns a task to each person. He gives to each one tastes and aptitudes appropriate to his special function. He directs one toward the contemplative life and another to teaching; this one to charitable works, that one to the foreign missions.

He varies His gifts indefinitely according to the times and the needs of His Church. Thus, for instance, the eremitical life, after flourishing for centuries, is almost gone. To free the Christians captured by the Moors, a famous order was founded that nowadays has no more reason for existing.[51] But new needs call for new forms of apostleship.

---

[50] Matt. 12:42.
[51] The Mercedarians, founded c. 1220 by St. Peter Nolasco.

We are beings who progress according to a directive idea peculiar to each. It is in view of this realization that God solicits us and urges us. To make us conform to our ideal and to develop our personality, He draws us to one or another virtue, to some special form of perfection, or some particular aspect of Christianity. How harmonious our lives would be if we collaborated with intelligence and docility, to correspond to His designs for each of us.

Some attractions of grace are still more particular. Witness a little shepherdess[52] conceiving the desire to free the French city of Orleans and to lead Charles VII to Rheims to have him crowned as king. Or consider St. John of God,[53] a merchant, pressed by the charity of Christ to found a hospital that would become the cradle of his order. Again, so many holy priests and valiant laymen had no rest until they had built a church or started a school, an orphanage, or a club.

Personal inspirations, like the commandments and the precepts, make known to us the will of God. But there is danger of illusion in such matters. Not to be abused by deceitful powers, we must reflect, we must accept advice, and we must pray.

Some supernatural attractions are merely transitory. God tests us. He ascertains our intentions. If He sees us ill-disposed, He does not insist. In other instances, He continues His entreaties during entire years. He solicits, He implores, and He

---

[52] St. Joan of Arc (1412-1431), French heroine who led the French army against English invaders.

[53] St. John of God (1495-1550), founder of the Order of Charity for the Service of the Sick.

threatens. He, as it were, besieges the soul, and again and again exhorts it.

⌒

God helps you to resist temptation

How many sinners have been pursued all their lives by a grace stronger than their wicked will! They fled from God as does an animal ferreted out. Fear of the renouncements demanded by their conscience impelled them to stifle remorse and even lose their faith so that they might sin more freely. But their conscience, although bribed, always protested. A divine light showed them the abyss open before them. They were obsessed, tormented, by a craving for conversion. At last they gave up, they cried for mercy, and on that prize long disputed, long desired, the divine Hunter has sung a triumphant hymn of victory.

Like attraction toward the good, aversion for evil may have a supernatural origin. On the verge of a fall, a sinner at times feels a restraining hand that stops him. An imperious voice forbids him to go further. What was a seduction for him yesterday has no more charm today; he is suddenly sobered. Whence comes this? Is it simply because the act he willed to accomplish appears to him now in its complex reality, with its aggravating circumstances, with all its dangerous consequences? Is it that he judges that act no more in the light of passion, but with his whole soul?

It has been said that the hand that acts is sometimes wiser than the mind that conceives the act. How many plans have been modified, how many projects abandoned, when the moment arrived to begin the action! But this rectification does not always occur. It happens most frequently that the spring once strained gets beyond control. Carried by his own outburst, a sinner jumps over all barriers and rushes toward self-gratification. If, therefore, at the point of acting, he has no more appetite for evil and renounces his guilty design, it is because God's grace has come, a grace for which he has to thank God's Providence.

⌒

God's consolations comfort and refresh you

To attach us to Him, God sometimes is lavish with spiritual delights. During periods of fervor, we do everything with pleasure; we find great sweetness in prayer, in pious readings, in Holy Communions, and even in the sacrifices that we impose upon ourselves for God. *Consolations* is the name given to such pure and sweet joys. They are given to us as a comfort. This earth is a vale of tears, where we expiate our personal faults and those of our ancestors. But one cannot suffer continuously. And so God's Providence manages to give us days of relaxation — and, as it were, in our ascent on the stairs that lead to Him, He supplies us with landing places where we can rest or breathe a little.

It is especially for the new converts, still frail and wavering, that He reserves His exquisite attentions. He wants to make them feel how sweet it is to serve Him. They are dealt with like the returning prodigal son.[54] How pleasant it must have been for him to wash his bleeding feet, to change his dirty rags for rich clothes, and to sit down at the banquet! The gaze of his old father enfolded him like a caress. So forsaken, so despised when far from home, he now felt he was forgiven,

[54] Cf. Luke 15:20-24.

rehabilitated, and beloved. Delicious hours were these. Later on he went to work like his older brother; he came to know the monotony of the daily effort, the fatigue, the weariness, and the disappointments. But at least for a few days, he was all joy. Thus his father willed to celebrate his return and, by this means, attract him to the farm.

Here is a passage of Fr. Faber wherein the consolations I mentioned are admirably pictured. No author I know of has described them with so much depth and poetry: "A chance text of Scripture falls upon the air, in church or out of it, and a touch of power comes with it, and with the power a flash of light, and a saint is made. There are brief sweetnesses in prayer, which come now and then in life, like shooting moonbeams through rents on close-packed, cloudy nights. They lit up the cross upon the steeple and were gone. But the soul fed on them for days. There are the first moments after Communion, an unearthly time, when we are like Mary carrying the Lord of Heaven and earth within her, and we feel Him, and have so much to say that we do not speak at all, and the time passes, and we seem to have missed an opportunity. But the work was done, and a supernatural heat is dancing in our blood, and straightway we climb a mountain on the road to Heaven.

"Then there are sudden gushes of love, and along with the love, light also; and we know not why they come nor whence. Heaven is all quiet above us, and makes no sign. Circumstances are going on around us in the old tame, languid way. What can it be? Certainly it came from within, as if a depth of the soul had broken up and flooded the surface; and we remember that, within us, in one of those depths, in which perhaps we ourselves have never been ourselves, and till eternity dawns, never shall be, God deigns to dwell, and now we understand the secret.

"Then there were momentary unions with Him in times of sorrow, which were so swift that they looked like possibilities rather than actual visitations. But they were true embraces from our heavenly Father, and they have healed us of diseases, and they have infused a new strength into us, and they were so close that we have been tingling ever since, and feel the pressure at this moment still."[55]

Sorrows and trials strengthen your soul

Our heart is like a keyboard, each key of which God strikes one after the other in succession. When He deems it opportune, He makes the sorrowful chords vibrate and draws from them great effects.

It is a well-known fact that a conversion is often preceded by a crisis of languor and weariness. The neophyte feels a strange uneasiness within him. A mysterious hand breaks one after the other the ties that bind him to the world, but not knowing how to come to himself, he wavers in anguish and distress, until the day when, discovering at last the only true good, he clings to it as to his only hope.

Once, while convalescing from illness, Francis of Assisi[56] went to sit down on a terrace that rose above the city. The

---

[55] Frederick William Faber, *The Creator and the Creature* (Baltimore: John Murphy and Company, 1857), 409.

[56] St. Francis of Assisi (c. 1182-1226), founder of the Franciscan Order.

scenery was splendid. From the heights of the blue sky, a beautiful light streamed on the Umbrian plains, but, to his great astonishment, Francis felt unmoved before such a spectacle. He experienced nothing of that joyful exaltation that convalescents or prisoners are wont to feel when, after being shut in for a long time, they look exhilaratingly on the clouds, the flowers, and the birds, and yearn to grasp the whole of nature. He attributed his coldness to the state of his health, but the cause was deeper. It was God Himself who pursued the soul of this young man and who, to draw him to Him, disenchanted him from the world. How many converts have felt the same salutary sadness, that deep disgust of all things, that restlessness of the heart until it is anchored to Him!

God, who afflicts sinners to correct them, does not spare His best friends. He wills to be loved for Himself, not for the consolations He gives. Therefore, He deprives the saintliest souls of any spiritual sweetness. He leaves them in dryness and desolation. They have the impression that they are forsaken. It seems to them that God averts from them His face and goes away — far away.

In the history of her life, St. Thérèse of Lisieux describes a trial of this kind. "I live" she says, "in a land of snow and fog. A great Prince has paid me a visit. He has spoken of His Kingdom — an earthly paradise — and has promised to lead me thither. But He has disappeared, and the sweet image He has engraved on my memory makes my exile unbearable. How cold and dark is this earth! It seems that an icy haze has penetrated into my heart. Between Heaven and me there is an impenetrable wall which ever gets taller and hides the stars from my eyes."

Under this discreet symbolic language, we may discern a profound anguish. Here is a young religious who, to follow her vocation, has given up the joys of a home and has renounced a brilliant future according to the world. And God, to whom she has sacrificed everything, forsakes her. She has sold everything to buy the precious pearl,[57] and this jewel slips from her. When she looks beyond the grave, it is not Heaven she sees, but darkness and emptiness.

And so it is in vain that she suffered — a cruel and terrible trial for such a frail child. And yet in that tempest, Thérèse did not lose courage. Having faith no more — I mean, feeling her faith no more — she went on working the works of faith. When the star that guided her had been eclipsed, she continued in the same direction, and by dint of walking in obscurity, she found again the light. Far from crushing her, this trial strengthened her. Her piety ripened in the midst of suffering.

While the Hebrews lived in the wilderness, a luminous pillar guided them during the night, and a celestial food sustained them during the day. Thus God not only enlightens our mind; He also stimulates and strengthens our will.

God's grace sustains you

That His help is indispensable is a truth of Faith confirmed by experience. What are we without Him? We are a fountain cut off from its reservoir and no longer giving water; a mechanism that remains motionless because it has no motive power of itself; or, to use a Gospel comparison, a branch cut off from the vine and quickly perishing.

---

[57] Cf. Matt. 13:46.

God's Providence Explained

It is God who operates within us the will to do, and gives us the means to do. Therefore, God's grace is necessary to move us to do good. Without divine help, we can neither pray, nor obtain the strength we need to resist temptations; we cannot even utter with faith the name of Jesus.

When God has inspired a resolution within us, we still need another grace to help us to hold to that resolution. We are like a little child who cannot walk alone. His father does not carry him in his arms, for he wishes to train him, but he helps him; if not, the child would fall at every step.

It is in the state of sin that one feels the absolute necessity of grace. There are some unhappy persons who are engulfed in deplorable habits of intemperance, impurity, or blasphemy. At certain hours of lucidity, they are aware of their misery. Like birds hit by the hunter's leaden bullet and fallen into the swamps, they flounder; they would like to get up, but their broken wings cannot lift them above the mud, and after vain efforts, they fall back into their abjection.

Without grace we can do nothing, but, with it, everything is possible. How many wonders it has worked in the saints of God! It has transformed timid men into heroes. Our martyrs have undergone the most cruel tortures with a constancy, a serenity, and a joy that dumbfounded their executioners. "They are bewitched," they said. "A charm keeps them unfeeling." God's grace was the mysterious charm that lifted them above themselves and made them partakers of God's infinite power.

How many times have we witnessed personally the efficacy of grace? Every time we have gone, absolved and purified, from the tribunal of Penance, we have felt an infusion of comfort and also of strength. At least for a few days, we more severely controlled ourselves; we were more assiduous in overcoming temptations or in running away from them. Grace acted within us — that grace which makes us live, and of which our mind, too much impregnated with rationalism, does not take sufficient account. When grace is in a nascent state, it works with full efficacy, and that is why, during the days that follow a good confession, it stirs us up and draws us; it is as a gentle breeze that uplifts the leaf and carries it where it wishes to go.

And what shall I say of the happy influence of the Holy Eucharist! Just as a substantial and abundant meal repairs our physical strength, so frequent and fervent Communion restores our soul and gives it an increase of energy. Such strength is not always made use of immediately, but it forms within us a reserve that we find at the moment of need and danger.

Recall your own intimate experience. Is it not true that more than once you have rejected temptations without knowing how or why? The Devil tried to seduce you by displaying to you the attractiveness of a guilty pleasure, and straightway, without reflecting on the motives of your refusal, you averted your head and replied to the advances of the tempter with an effective "No!" Whence came such a decision, which perhaps astonished you? It came from God's grace accumulated in you by your past Communions and which, without your knowing it, intervened at the opportune moment.

Grace is obtained also by prayer. There is no true prayer that is not answered. When we ask for temporal favors — health, wealth, success — God sometimes refuses them. It is our sanctification that He has in view, not the satisfying of our earthly desires. But if, instead of a miserable good that would lead to our perdition, He gives us an increase of virtue and piety — a priceless treasure — we cannot complain. He grants us more than we desired and asked for.

Again, grace is often given to us without any request on our part. In the midst of our ordinary tasks or recreations, during our meals and our sleep, God's Providence watches over us, removing dangers and, as it were, putting into our hands what we need. At every moment, it intervenes in our spiritual life. Every time we have a movement of charity or a spontaneous impulse toward goodness, it is God who leads us to it.

☞

You draw life from Christ

This truth will appear with more clearness if we remind ourselves of St. Paul's teaching concerning the union of Christ and the faithful. We are the cells of a vast organism of which Christ is the soul. He inspires, directs, and vivifies us.

Our spiritual life is, therefore, a partnership. And so true is this that we do not have the right to glory in our own good works. They are only partly ours. The grape is yielded by the branch, but the sap, which feeds the branch, comes from the roots and is transmitted through the stem; it is thus the product of the whole plant. Therefore, our good works are the fruit of a continuous and intimate collaboration between Christ and us.

According to Pantheists, we are modes of the divine substance. In the universe, there is only one autonomous activity. It is God who thinks, desires, and acts in us. That is an impious doctrine, which, in suppressing freedom and responsibility, justifies any turpitude and any crime. But if it is untrue to say that God does all in us, it is another error to pretend that we can dispense with Him.

The Savior then spoke truly when He said, "I am the life."[58] He is the full, fertile, inexhaustible life from which our life derives its origin and power. From Him come our salvation, our perfection, and our happiness. At first glance, it seems that each of us is sufficient unto himself. Have we not the free choice of our career and our acts?

There are also people who, gulled by their vanity, claim complete autonomy and pretend to depend on nobody. Fools! They have not reflected on the exigencies of our nature; they know not on what numerous and varied conditions our spiritual life depends. In looking at a beautiful tree, one might think that it owes its vigor to the vital principle that animates it. This is true, but the subterranean water from which the roots drink has provided it with strength to develop its stately boughs. Let that hidden source get dry or change its course, and the tree will wither as it stands. In the same manner, our individual life has its roots plunged into the Infinite. Apparently it is our own property and our work, but dig deeper, and you will find the deep source from which it emanates.

⌒

God wills or permits all that happens

In his *Christian Meditations*, French philosopher Nicolas Malebranche tells us that nature sometimes favors the action of grace and sometimes hinders it. "Bad weather, sickness, or some whimsical reason prevents a libertine from calling on the object of his sinful passion; since his concupiscence is not just now excited, a degree of grace which would have no effect in other circumstances is now able to convert him. On the

[58] John 14:6.

other hand, So-and-So was moved enough by God's grace to wish to make restitution of stolen goods; but at the last moment, the incidental, casual presence of his child has awakened paternal love and has led him not to effect restitution."

Although these comparisons may appear somewhat fair, the philosopher's interpretation is quite dangerous. By *nature*, Malebranche means the necessary sequel of a first movement impressed on the mass of atoms. According to him, after having created material substances, God would have given to them a certain impulse operative for all time, and everything would then be explained by this initial movement: the ray of the sun that gives me light, the wind that whispers at my window, and even the wanderings of that butterfly which flits from flower to flower. But if, for sake of simplicity, God had created a nature able to oppose His action, He would have limited and contradicted Himself, which indeed is an impossibility. Undoubtedly He proceeds most simply, and His laws are general, but He has foreseen and calculated even their least effects. It is He who has told us through His Son: "Are not five sparrows sold for two farthings, and not one of them is forgotten before God. Yea, the very hairs of your head are all numbered."[59]

True Christians — those who have not only the Faith, but also the spirit of Faith — are permeated with that Gospel teaching. When an accident happens, they attribute it, not to ill luck (there is no such thing) nor to the sport of natural forces, but to Him who, in creating the causes, has contrived all their effects. Shot accidentally by a clumsy hunter, Baron

[59] Matt. 10:29-30.

de Chantal[60] said to the poor innocent hunter, "It is God's deed rather than thine." Such admirable language of Christian resignation seems nearer the truth than the consideration of Malebranche and his successors.

And so nothing happens, not even the death of a bird nor the fall of a hair, that has not been permitted or willed by God's Providence. Some of such numberless events manifest God's justice, as, for instance, the punishments that even here below are inflicted on impenitent sinners; others occur for our sanctification and our salvation. Hence it follows that he who faithfully works for his own soul and for God walks according to divine direction; the winds and the stars are for Him; all things concur with His designs.

There are facts, however, that, because of their impact on our moral life, compel us to face them more closely. Their divine mark is, as it were, visible to the naked eye. We shall speak of these and see how they favor the interior action of grace.

⌒

God works through miracles

First, let us consider miraculous events — and first, the conversion of St. Paul. A fact of capital importance this is. If the nascent Church had been recruited merely from the Jewish people, her development would have been slow. If the Apostles had imposed legal observances — circumcision, for instance — on the pagans, they would have discouraged many neophytes. St. Paul saw and destroyed this twofold obstacle.

[60] The husband of St. Jane Frances de Chantal (1572-1641), foundress of the Visitation Order.

Boldly he cut the tie that attached the Church to the synagogue and led her toward the pagan nations. An immense field was now open; the Church's future was assured.

Again, what strikes us in the conversion of the Apostle of the Gentiles is the miraculous element. How did this young Pharisee, so stubborn in his belief and so set against the new Faith, suddenly transform himself into an apostle of Christ? Many natural explanations have been proposed: a storm, a sunstroke, an epileptic disease — ridiculous hypotheses, good for those to whom the worst absurdities are more credible than miracles. The truth is that to understand what happened on the way to Damascus we have to look Heavenward. The light shining around Saul, the voice speaking to him, the blindness cured by the prayer of Ananias, the complete change in the soul of the Pharisee — all these things are of a supernatural order. The apostle had many reasons to say, "By the grace of God I am what I am."[61] On this "vessel of election,"[62] the divine Worker indeed left His fingerprints.

Miracles are facts unforeseen, rare, conspicuous. But usually the divine action hides itself in a series of secondary causes. It is so discreet that it passes unnoticed, although it is universal and constant. It is like the sun, which does not always shine, but even when veiled by clouds, ever sends us light and heat.

⌒

God works through ordinary events

To sanctify and save us, God sometimes uses events that are seemingly insignificant, but are fraught with considerable

---

[61] 1 Cor. 15:10.
[62] Acts 9:15.

consequences, as, for instance, the little incident that brought about the conversion of St. Augustine.[63] Urged by God's grace, he thought of embracing the Christian Faith, but, like many others, he ever procrastinated. One day, while he meditated in a garden, he heard a child saying in a singing voice, "*Tolle, lege,*" that is, "Take up and read." Startled by such a strange order, Augustine opened a book and read the passage that first appeared. It was this text of St. Paul: "Not in rioting and drunkenness, not in chambering and impurities, not in contention and envy; but put ye on the Lord Jesus Christ, and make not provision for the flesh in its concupiscences."[64] Augustine read no further, nor was there need. He renounced his sinful life and began to march along the road that leads to God. His case is far from unique in the history of souls.

For thirty years, the Son of God hid Himself at Nazareth as a young working man. Today again He is hidden in the tabernacle under the appearance of bread. Thus, the deeds of God conceal themselves sometimes under ordinary events so humble as not to attract attention. We are far from thinking that they are a divine visitation. But with the warmth they bring within us, their origin reveals itself. We then turn back to greet Him who sends them, but God has passed, and from afar we perceive only the fringe of His vestment of light.

Who would not admire how closely and carefully God prepares His apostolic workers? He calls each from his mother's womb.[65] He selects his family and the place of his birth. He

---

[63] St. Augustine (354-430), Bishop of Hippo.

[64] Rom. 13:13.

[65] Cf. Jer. 1:5.

places him in a favorable environment. He molds his character. At the decisive hours of his life, He hands him the book that he must read. He entrusts him to a priest whose words forewarn and forearm him. To lead him where He wants him to go, He uses his natural dispositions. He turns everything to account, even his sins. What foresight on His part in all this! To save a soul, God seems to display as much wisdom as to redeem a world. And no wonder, since He acts according to His nature and is all in all His works.

Certain events merely propose the divine will, in giving us the facility to accomplish a good work. A beggar knocks at our door, a friend asks for advice, a great sermon is preached in our town — these are so many occasions to do good and to sanctify. Oftentimes also, God imposes His will upon us and places us in the presence of an accomplished fact. Events occur in which we have no part, but which modify our situation and demand new duties. "Could we see the masters whom God gives us," says Pascal, "how merrily we would obey them! Necessity and events are such masters."

～

Some events compel you to obey God's will

Yes, some events are masters, and masters in the full meaning of the word — *magistri et domini,* masters that teach and command. They clearly signify the will of God.

Hesitation is possible when we have to deal with a mere opportunity. Suppose a neighbor is ill and destitute. It may so happen that others will help him. But necessity does not leave us in doubt; it grasps us with an iron hand and draws us toward the road we must take. We are stricken with an incurable disease or a grave infirmity; we have to give up our work and sternly accept the stern will of God. A war is declared, we are mobilized, and we must go. In all such cases, there is nothing to discuss; the voice of conscience is clear and imperious.

Another benefit that comes from such events is to remind us forcibly of certain truths. They teach us in a manner that is both brief and striking. Better than discourses, the death of a relative or a reverse in fortune makes us feel how short is life and how unstable are all human affairs. And what a stern master is war! How many illusions it dispels; how many false ideas it corrects! How it demonstrates the necessity of discipline!

⌒

God provides others to teach and comfort you

Many of the events that concern us are caused by men. Our greatest pains and our greatest joys come from our fellowmen, who are instruments used by God to edify, comfort, and exercise us.

In the first line of providential agents, there is the priest. In him, Christ renews His humanity. What He had done personally during the years of His mortal life, He now does every day through the lips and the hands of His ministers. He goes on preaching His gospel. Ever merciful, He heals human souls and brings to them spiritual life. On the altar, as on Calvary, He sacrifices Himself and gives Himself as our food. How grateful we must be to the dispensers of so great a mystery! The poor bless the charitable hands that give them bread; the sick bless the skillful hands that nurse them; how much more we must bless the priestly hands that every day, if such is our wish, bring us God's grace and God Himself, who is the principle of grace!

We have to be thankful also to the Religious and to all those who, according to their strength and means, work for the extension of God's kingdom. Since we are part and parcel of the Mystical Body of Christ, the Church, His interest is our own interest. We have special obligations to those who consciously or not have been good to us. Through their words, their writings, or their examples, many have edified us without knowing it. Thousands of persons have contributed to our formation who will know only on the Last Day how serviceable they have been to us.

A comforting thought this is. We are discouraged at times to see the small results of our labors. Are we sure, absolutely sure, that we have saved one single soul? We are not and cannot be. But this must not discourage us. Our influence is perhaps more efficacious than it seems. A poet has said:

> As on the smooth expanse of crystal lakes
> The sinking stone at first a circle makes;
> The trembling surface by the motion stirred,
> Spreads in a second circle, then a third;
> Wide, and more wide, the floating rings advance,
> Fill all the watery plain, and to the margin dance.[66]

So the souls made better by our influence make others better, too. The light that we have emitted is reflected in a series of mirrors that send one to another the ray of which we are the focus.

It happens also that in days of trouble, unknown people call on us and set us at ease. Whence do they come? How and why do they take interest in us? There is no need to know, but there is need to thank God's Providence for it.

---

[66] Alexander Pope, "Temple of Flame," line 436.

Again, we may look upon our relatives and friends as God's agents. Their affection is very precious to us, for it answers a need of our nature. But how mistaken we are if we blindly lean upon them. They are God's creatures as we are. Only our Creator can satisfy us fully. Our best friends are imperfect; by and by, their defects appear and hurt our heart.

What is said by Jeremiah — "Cursed be the man that trusteth in man"[67] — is said by God and therefore cannot be contested. But it reproves only that human confidence which ignores God and denies His all-powerful faithfulness. And the context shows it, for after having said, "Cursed be the man that trusteth in man," the prophet adds immediately, "and maketh flesh his arm, and whose heart departeth from the Lord; he shall be like heat in the desert, and shall not see when good cometh, but shall inhabit the parched places in the wilderness, in a salt land, and not inhabited. Blessed is the man that trusteth in the Lord, and whose hope the Lord is; for he shall be as a tree planted by the waters, and that spreadeth out its roots by the river, and shall not see when heat cometh, but his leaf shall be green."[68]

St. Thomas gives us here a golden rule: "It is certainly not permitted to hope in men, or in any creature whatever, as if they were the first cause which could lead us to beatitude. We may nevertheless put our hope in men, as in secondary agents, and as instruments able to help us to obtain the blessings which are co-ordained to our end. Men are but the instruments whereby God Himself loves us. All true excellence in

[67] Jer. 17:5.
[68] Jer. 17:5-8.

them which excites our hope is a partial aspect of the divine Beauty, which they mirror. It is God in them that we love; it is God who loves us in them."[69] Hence, our confidence in the saints of Heaven and our prayers to them; hence, also, our confidence in the saints of this earth, since in a large measure God dwells and works in them, and with the evident design of acting through them on their brethren.

☞

God uses even persecution to bring about good

Even our personal enemies and the persecutors of the Church are God's instruments to test and try us. Well known is that passage of the Holy Scriptures often quoted by the theologians: "And now I have given all these lands into the hand of Nabuchodonosor, King of Babylon, my servant."[70] In what sense was this pagan king a servant of the true God? He was not a voluntary servant, but God made use of him. God had chosen him from all eternity to be the minister of His chastisements.

It is from the same viewpoint that the four Evangelists consider the enemies of Christ. We are sometimes astonished in seeing how cold they are in their account of the Passion of our Savior — no anger, no indignation, not one condemnatory word about Judas or Pilate. It is because the inspired writers have faith in Providence. They know that all the details of the Passion had been planned to humiliate the Son of God. Since Jesus willed to be betrayed and unjustly condemned, there had to be a Judas and a Pilate. Assuredly, Judas and Pilate were

---

[69] Cf. St. Thomas Aquinas, *Summa Theologica*, II-II, Q. 17, art. 4.
[70] Jer. 27:6.

gravely guilty, since they acted against their conscience, but nonetheless they played a necessary part in the tragedy of Calvary.

We may now understand the reason the Gospels command us to love our enemies. We must pray for those who persecute us, not only so that we may obey the divine Master and follow His example, but also because persecutors contribute (unconsciously as it may be) to the work of our sanctification. A persecution is a storm that commits ravages, but withal carries away the dry leaves and strengthens the roots of the trees. To resist the tempest, we must pray with fervor as though everything depended on God, and we must work as though everything depended on us. Calles,[71] the modern Nero, was rightly called "the great organizer of Catholic forces in Mexico."

☞

God has put nature at your service

God, sovereign Master of all things, has set at our service the inferior creatures. He said to our first parents, "Fill the earth and subdue it, and rule over the fishes of the sea, and the fowls of the air, and all living creatures that move upon the earth."[72] By this divine mandate, we have been appointed kings of the whole creation. Ours are all plants and animals, and it is because they are ours that they charm and please us.

Even the pagans felt the charm of nature. So beautiful it was to them that they looked upon it as divine. One of the greatest sanctuaries of the world, in Heliopolis, was dedicated

---

[71] Plutarco Elías Calles (1877-1945), President of Mexico who persecuted the Church.

[72] Gen. 1:28.

to the sun, and there the source of light was given divine honors. A sacrilegious homage it was, since the creature was adored instead of the Creator.

But Christians enlightened by Faith take care not to pay to the work the tribute that is due to the Worker. To us, nature attests God's authorship of all things. How enthusiastically our poets sing of it! Is there a more beautiful hymn than this addressed by St. Francis to his brother the Sun?

> I bless Thee, Father, that where'er I go
> A brotherhood of blessed creatures goes
> With me, and biddeth me godspeed. For all
> Thy mute and innocent creatures take my thanks:
> To me they are child-brethren without speech or sin.
> And first for him, the noblest of them all,
> He who brings day and summer, disenchants
> The icebound streams, and wakes the happy birds,
> Pure choristers, to matins; at whose call
> The young flowers, startled from their hiding places,
> Peep and laugh; who clothes the earth and fills
> The heavens with joy; and he is beautiful
> And radiant with great splendor. Praise to Thee,
> O Highest, for our royal brother Sun;
> For bears he not an impress, Lord, of Thee?

In our own being, we find other witnesses of God's Providence. Our body is composed of numberless cells, each one of them seemingly acting for itself. And yet they are submitted to a common law and combine to form a unit. Silent workers, they ever form or repair our tissues and fight the parasites that enter into us with the air we breathe and the food we eat. Each one of us governs a populous city that in its complexity could be compared to the universe.

⁀

God calls you to work with Him

The consequence of divine activity we find ever and everywhere. This thought that seems to be our concept has been discreetly inspired by God; like a shooting star, as it were, it has passed in the sky of our soul, but it came from Him. This resolution that we have taken after ripe deliberation is the result of God's grace. The course of events weighs upon us; it has its share in our vocation and our moral formation. It is God who directs it. Without doing violence to our liberty, He maneuvers us and leads us according to His will.

As St. Paul says, "We are God's fellow workers."[73] We labor, but not alone; and clever is he who can distinguish in our activity the part of our personal effort, and the part of divine grace. We are like farmers: the harvest depends on the care with which we plough the ground, sow the seed, hoe, dig, cultivate, and clean; but it depends also on the weather and finally on God's good pleasure.

The important thing for us is to submit ourselves to God's grace. There is nothing more beautiful under the sun than a life ordained by divine wisdom.

[73] 1 Cor. 3:9 (Revised Standard Version).

Chapter Three

God's ways will surprise you

God is infinite in wisdom, in power, and in love. Man is finite and limited; a miserable creature, he is, however, endowed with the noble privilege to obey God or to disobey Him. This is an elementary truth that we must not lose sight of when we study the way in which God governs men.

God acts according to His nature, which is so different from ours. There is in His conduct something that is surprising and disconcerting at first glance. On the other hand, His action adapts itself to the object with which it deals. He turns everything to account; He makes use of our inclinations; He tempers the wind according to our weakness; and He respects our dignity. Several of His ways of acting are thus explained. As soon as we see their secret reason, our surprise is changed into admiration, and we wind up praising Him for all things.

But we cannot understand every part of God's way of governing us. Our sounding line is too short to reach the bottom of the mystery. After having explored it as far as possible, there comes a moment when it floats above the abyss.

It is wise, then, to stop and to cry out with St. Paul, "Oh, the depth of the riches of the wisdom and of the knowledge of God! How incomprehensible are His judgments, and how unsearchable His ways! For who hath known the mind of the Lord? Or who hath been His counselor? Or who hath first given to Him, and recompense shall be made him? For of Him, and by Him, and in Him, are all things. To Him be glory for ever. Amen."[74]

The ways of God are not our ways. Their air of strangeness and their apparent anomaly are what first strike us. Some of them seem contrary to the end that God has in view. His will is our happiness, our sanctification, and our salvation. Why, then, does He inflict suffering on us? Why does He permit temptation and sin?

We strive to spare our friends any pain. How happy they would be if our power were equal to our love! And if we were the rulers of nature, our first care would be to eliminate war, sorrow, and death.

Thus argue many superficial souls who, lowering God to their level, lend Him their worldly preoccupations and efforts. They are amazed when they see Him do exactly the contrary of what they would do. Vexed and provoked, they murmur and blaspheme. To take their revenge on God, who afflicts them, they deprive Him of their homage. Others lose their faith in a God who does not condescend to stoop to their whims.

Astonished by the defeats of St. Louis,[75] the Saracens said to their prisoners, "We would reject Mohammed if he did not help us." So also, at times, is the cry of Christians. To them religion is good only insofar as it favors their temporal prosperity. They look upon God as a Protector of whom they make use, not as a Master whom they must serve at all costs. To them everything is subordinate to the present life.

---

[74] Rom. 11:33-36.
[75] St. Louis IX (1214-1270), King of France.

⌒

Suffering is an effective remedy

God has other views. Before all, He seeks His glory. Radiant Sun of the world, He wills to reflect Himself in numberless creatures able to love Him eternally. He wills to fill His home of Heaven with adorers. His design, therefore, is not to make us happy here below, but to sanctify us.

Now, what is a saint? A saint is a man whose law is the good pleasure of God and whose ambition is to possess Him someday. Hence, it follows that the greatest obstacle to sanctity is an exaggerated attachment to ourselves or to other creatures. To break down such obstacles, God, always wise and powerful, sends us suffering — a bitter, a violent remedy, a necessary remedy.

• *Suffering averts us from false joys.* We are fascinated by earthly things. We know and we admit that it is wiser to think less of time than of eternity, and yet we let ourselves be tempted to forget such truth. We are like children more moved by the brightness of one electric light than by the splendor of the stars.

To break the charm that captivates us, God pours poison into our false joys; into the cup of illicit pleasures He pours shame, disgust, and remorse. As we snatch a knife from a child's hand, God takes from us the gold that to us was a source of confidence, or friends who were too dear. He deprives us of our health, without which there is no rejoicing. Guests who have no appetite, we sit at a table loaded with foods that merely disgust us. Then our eyes are open; we understand the littleness of life, and our soul, freed from delusion, thinks of a better world where nothing will disturb its joy.

• *Suffering enlightens us.* Suffering does in the moral order what night does in the physical order. When the sun has disappeared behind the horizon, shadows invade the valleys and the plains; darkness covers the sky, but beyond the veil, we see the stars. These worlds swirling in limitless spaces lift up our thoughts to prodigious heights, above all mundane anxieties, into serene regions where they freely unfold themselves. Night, which brings us refreshing sleep and forgetfulness, brings us, or rather revives, the feeling of infinitude. Yes, night is good.

Good also is suffering. It covers this land of exile with thick shadows, and so it dissipates many dreams and illusions. But as this world darkens, the truths of Faith appear nearer and more evident. When mirth decays and dies and when all things lose their charm, we instinctively lift the eyes of our soul to the supernatural lights.

• *Suffering reveals to us our faults and leads us to correct them.* Deceived by self-love, we misjudge our intentions. We are under the impression that we are doing good to others when we are merely striving to do good to ourselves; and we would remain in such dangerous illusion if failures, which are God's warnings, did not invite us to examine ourselves.

We read in Holy Scriptures that, to punish a heinous crime committed by the Benjamites, eleven tribes of

Israel entered into a league and declared war on the of-
fenders. Although much more numerous than their
foes, the sons of Israel were twice defeated. They then
consulted the Lord to know whether they should again
fight the children of Benjamin. And the Lord answered
them, "Go up against them, and join battle." The next
day, there was a new battle and a new defeat. What was
the reason for such humiliation to men who were the
champions of justice? Pride was their sin. They trusted
in their strength and their number more than in God's
help. Before attempting to punish a crime, they ought
to have examined themselves and asked pardon for their
own sins. Enlightened by misfortune, they repented;
they fasted and offered sacrifices. Now again, they consulted the Lord, and the Lord said to them, "Go up, for
tomorrow I will deliver your enemy into your hands."
The next day, the Benjamites were defeated.[76]

• *Suffering strengthens us.* Our being, which is limited,
but so complex and so rich, has possibilities of which we
are seldom aware; buried in it are treasures that necessity alone leads us to discover. Sometimes, in the midst
of a storm, mariners have to stay continuously on the
deck for days, with scarcely any food or sleep, struggling
for their lives. The instinct of self-preservation exalts
their courage and leads them to heroism. Before the
Great War, who could have thought that soldiers would
be able to bear for years the burden of the heat and the

[76] Judg. 20.

cold, the rain and the snow, the pain, the filth, and the horror? But they bore all these things to save their honor and their independence. In all cases, it is the fear of suffering that withdraws man from moral mediocrity, increases his strength, and compels him to outdo himself.

• *Suffering is the great incentive of spiritual life.* If we were always satisfied with ourselves, we would not be able to progress at all. We would be so stationary as to become parts of the landscape. But God, who desires our sanctification, does not give us such rest. He presses and urges us to march forward. To shake our indolence, He sends us tribulations and trials. We then feel poor and dejected. It is a crisis, painful always, but usually ripening into progress.

• *The greatest benefit of suffering, patiently accepted, is to conform us to our divine Master.* Jesus is the only man of whom God has said, "This is my beloved Son in whom I am well pleased."[77] He is the perfect man, the man according to the heart of God. He alone is great; He alone is pure. Yet how poor and little He appears! He, the Son of the living God, has met with fatigue, deceptions, contempt, betrayal, persecution, and death. But far from dimming His glory, His humiliations render Him the more splendid to our eyes. They have made Him more agreeable to God and more beloved by men. Having voluntarily charged Himself with our iniquities,

[77] Matt. 3:17.

He was the substitute of sinners — He, the great Penitent. To fulfill His mission, He took from the day of His birth the attitude and the feeling that behoove a repentant sinner: the spirit of penance, complete humility, and love of the hidden life.

It follows, then, that we find favor in the eyes of our heavenly Father according to the proportion in which we are like His divine Son. Every day, we mark ourselves with the Sign of the Cross to remind ourselves that we are the disciples of a crucified God.

Now, the disciple is not above his Master:[78] he must imitate Him in His Passion if he wishes to participate in His triumph. It is truly said that suffering is a mark of predestination. When God wants to save a soul, He calls it, He justifies it, He conforms it to the image of His Son. And none is conformed to our Lord Jesus Christ who does not carry the Cross as He did.

꣠

*God's blessings are often
mistaken for punishments*

Since suffering is good and necessary, no wonder God inflicts it upon sinners so that they may be converted, and upon the just so that they may be more sanctified. God is good; His goodness transcends our imagination. But it is precisely because of His goodness that He sends us trials. He feels no false pity or cruel compassion. If a surgeon sees his son in danger and in need of being operated upon, he does not hesitate to use the knife; delay in such a case would be guilty and even

[78] John 13:16.

75

criminal. God acts likewise. He tries us, but His trials are for the good of our immortal soul.

Anyone seeing the mother of Moses hide him in the reeds by the river's brink would have been indignant at her. And yet such action was inspired by love — tender, strong, and wise love. She went away lest she awaken suspicion, but she left her daughter near the river to watch the newborn baby. In exposing him to danger, she saved his life, and prepared a magnificent future for him.[79]

Thus God is never nearer to us than when He seems to be far from us. We fancy that He abandons us, and He is sustaining us. We complain that He is impoverishing us, and He is enriching us. His refusals are favors; His apparent punishments are in reality His greatest benefits.

Since suffering is both prophylactic and curative, no wonder the Divine Physician applies such an efficacious remedy to us. But why does He not avert from us the danger of losing our eternal salvation?

꒰

Temptations combat self-love

Holy Scripture tells us that God is not the author of temptations. It is by our own concupiscence that we are tempted and allured to evil. Because of our original fall in Adam and Eve, there has been within us an inversion of values, so that we dislike what we ought to like, and we like what we ought to dislike. The flowers of a day have more attraction for us than the fruits that endure. It is true that God's grace stabilizes such lack of equilibrium, but it does not suppress it. The blood of

[79] Exod. 2:3 ff.

Jesus, who has redeemed us, has not re-established us in our primitive integrity, and God does not perform a continuous miracle to curb the desires of our senses. The cause of our temptations, therefore, is first the depravity of our nature.

"God tempteth no man."[80] He does, however, allow us to be tempted in order to mortify our self-love. There is no vice that He detests more than pride. Pride, indeed, is a sin against nature, for it supposes a complete denial of normal relations between God and man.

Miserable littleness that we are, we can do nothing without divine help. We cannot form one good desire; we cannot even move our lips to utter a prayer. To believe that we are self-sufficient and to attribute merit to our own works is to be both mistaken and unjust; it is to steal a ray from the divine glory and place it on ourselves. God welcomes the repentant publican with joyful mercy, but from the Pharisee infatuated with himself He turns away in anger.[81]

But how can self-love be lessened? Temptation assuredly is one of the most efficacious means. Nothing makes us feel our innate corruption more than this unsought-for attraction to evil. When somewhat strong and lasting, temptation provokes within us a strange disturbance. It changes our ideas and our ways of seeing things. What yesterday seemed a sin now appears as a source of pleasure; what we held in horror a while ago now fascinates us. Many do not resist such attraction!

Oh, the shameful misery of our nature! It is not enough that we are solicited by the Devil and the world. These

[80] Cf. James 1:13.
[81] Cf. Luke 18:10-14.

enemies of our salvation find accomplices even in our heart, hallowed by the waters of Baptism!

Another advantage of temptation is to make us understand the truth of this word of Christ: "Without me you can do nothing."[82] Without God's grace, it is utterly impossible for us to be victorious in our struggles. Some people become dizzy when standing on the edge of a precipice. They feel as if everything whirled around them. Their head swims; drops of sweat pearl on their faces. They cling to the trees, to the rocks, to anything they can grasp. And yet they cannot draw away their eyes from the abyss that terrifies them. They are as though sucked by an air current, and they fall if some passerby does not come to help them. Thus, in the throes of temptation, when the heart is perturbed and the imagination on fire, we fall if we do not pray to the Lord.

It is for this reason — because temptation teaches us our weakness and the necessity of prayer — that temptation spares no one, not even the saints.

How many surprising revelations we find on this subject in hagiography! In spite of his mortification, his spirit of poverty, and his detachment from all things, St. Francis of Assisi felt the sting of covetousness. St. Jane Frances de Chantal said that her soul was like a park infested with impure animals. Not even old age is safe from temptation. "I am eighty-eight years old," St. Alphonsus Liguori[83] admitted, "and I feel within me all the fire of youth."

---

[82] John 15:5.

[83] St. Alphonsus Liguori (1696-1787), moral theologian and founder of the Redemptorists.

Why does God permit such humiliating temptations? Precisely because they are humiliating. More than others, the saints have to guard against the snares of self-love. On the heights of their holiness, they commit only slight sins; they perform wonderful works and exercise a beneficent influence over humanity; some of them walk far along the mystical ways. They are in danger of becoming a prey to pride. "Rejoice that you have at last arrived at such lofty degrees of sanctity," the Devil tells them. Woe to them if, listening to such flattery, they take delight in themselves! To obviate such danger and to offset the favors He gives them, God sends them the trial that St. Paul underwent even after his ecstasies. Read the very words of this apostle: "Lest the greatness of the revelations should exalt me, there was given me a sting of my flesh, an angel of Satan to buffet me. For which thing, thrice I besought the Lord that it might depart from me. And He said to me, 'My grace is sufficient for thee': for power is made perfect in infirmities . . . that the power of Christ may dwell in me."[84]

Those who claim that they can dispense with God face temptation with only the strength of their own will — a feeble breakwater, which soon yields to the urge of passions and habits. But the lowly ones who distrust themselves beg for God's grace, which makes them partakers of His infinite power. The consciousness of our frailty leads us to God, who comes to our help. It is, therefore, from our weakness that our strength arises.

Still more than temptation, sin humiliates us. When again and again we have broken our promises to God, when for years

[84] 2 Cor. 12:7-9.

we have approached the holy tribunal of Penance with the same weight of sins, then we feel that at last we must renew our efforts to be watchful and prayerful. A sin wounds you; it also warns you.

Behold Peter, the first chief of the Church. He swears faithfulness and fealty to Christ, and a few hours later he denies his Master. A lamentable fall this was, but one that, far from lessening his spiritual progress, accelerated it. The experience of his frailty caused this apostle to be less presumptuous and less imprudent. Like Mary of Magdala, he loved Him much who forgave him so much.[85] He willed to show himself worthy of His confidence and atoned his moment of sin by a whole life consecrated to apostleship and crowned by martyrdom. "To them that love God, all things work together unto good,"[86] said St. Paul. "Even sins," rejoined St. Augustine.

But let us not forget: it is only in those who love God that sin produces such a salutary reaction. They trip and fall, by accident, by excitement. Sin now and then seduces them, but it remains hateful to them. Their main desire is to please God and save their souls. They are quite different from those who have not even the faint, imperfect volition of conversion and who establish themselves in sin — each new sin soiling them and causing them to sink deeper and deeper into the mire.

Persecution strengthens the Church

Sin is evil, and so is persecution. God does not authorize it, but He permits it for the welfare of the faithful. Since the

---

[85] Cf. Luke 7:47.
[86] Rom. 8:28.

Church has no weapons with which to resist violence, it seems that God should have set her under the safeguard of civil power. He tempers the wind to the shorn lamb. He opens His hand and fills every living creature. He could have given human protection to her who is His living voice on earth. "Ah!" we say. "If the action of the Church were favored by the governments of the world, if she had at her service the great forces of finance, press, and politics, how rapidly she would spread. All infidels would be converted in a short time. She would create concord and harmony between all nations, and human society would be a universal brotherhood."

But this is a childish illusion, a utopian dream. God's Providence knows our needs better than we do. In the course of ages, at times, there has been union between Church and state. Theoretically, it is a consummation devoutly to be wished, but, practically, it has never worked.

How many Caesars have wished their services repaid by making the Church a tool for their ambition! How many hypocrites have affected external piety merely to be seen and admired! How many Christians, seeing the Church so prosperous, have failed to fight for her!

On the other hand, in the days of trial, the true servants of Christ work and wrestle for the defense of their Faith. They want to fill up the spaces made empty by the desertion of renegades and apostates. They want to console Christ for the outrages He receives. They want to adore Him for those who blaspheme Him. They want to love Him for those who hate Him. They want to serve Him for those who forsake Him. But so grave is the peril, and so frightful are the powers of Hell, that their only hope is in the help from above. The very danger they are in refreshes their supernatural thoughts and renews their piety.

"How beautiful is the Church when she is sustained only by God," said Pascal. And Bossuet[87] who, living under the regime of a protectorate, knew the abuses thereof, appreciated the times of persecutions: "If sufferings are necessary to sustain the spirit of Christianity, Lord, give us back the Domitians and the Neros."

Witnesses of the ruins that the enemies of the Church have heaped up in France, Mexico, and Russia, we dare not express such wishes. It is nonetheless true that persecutions have happy harvests; the grass, when mown, grows more thick and more green. God does not spare this trial when He deems it useful.

The history of His Church is a *via dolorosa*, a veritable Way of the Cross. She is always in agony; at times she seems to be dying; her exulting enemies say among themselves that her end is in view. But their thought of triumph comes too soon; what they take for the death knell is nothing else but the gladsome chiming that brings the tidings of a resurrection.

We now see why God's Providence chooses means that seem contrary to the end in view. It is because, in fact, such means are best. The way to Heaven lies along the brink of a precipice. Every moment we may fall; we are safe only if we are upheld by God's hand. To distrust ourselves and to trust in God's grace must be our disposition. And if so, since so, how good is God to keep us close to danger.

---

[87] Jacques Bénigne Bossuet (1627-1704), French preacher and Bishop of Meaux.

⌒

God's infinite love is unsearchable

"Lord," queried the ancient patriarch, "hast Thou eyes of flesh? Or shalt Thou see as man seeth?"[88] God sees from on high and from afar. He sees not as we see; His wisdom, infinitely superior to ours, reaches its aim by means we cannot dream of. Add to this that His love, as infinite as His knowledge, carries Him to excesses that both confound and enrapture us.

Man is man: he loves with his heart — a heart narrow usually, limited always. God also loves according to His nature, but as His nature is infinite, His love is infinitely great. We cannot here below have any idea of such love. Even when purest and deepest and most intense, human love is but the merest shadow of divine love — the love that God bestows on the least soul in the state of grace.

Does this mean that there is nothing common between divine love and ours? I do not go so far as that. What is found in the effect is found in the cause, at least in seed form. Since our love is a participation of God's love, one and the other have the same essence and obey the same laws. I speak, of course, of true love, unselfish love, not of that egoistic and sensual emotion (call it passion if you will) which strives to cull pleasure from any living flower and casts it aside with disdain or anger when it has ceased to bloom.

Such love as God has placed in our heart is His also and to the highest degree. "In a thousand places of Holy Writ," Bernard Dalgairns says, "God points to the awful strength and the yearning depth of human love, and bids us remember that His

---

[88] Job 10:4.

own is the same infinitely intensified. We may draw conclusions, therefore, from our love to His, and we are quite safe in asserting that, as the love of the mother for her child is something far deeper and more tender than pity, so, when God says that He is the great lover of souls, He does not mean simple compassion and benevolence, but true and real love. Now, love ever tends to union, and we may be sure that the love of God is an ineffable desire of the closest union with our souls."

The climax of such divine love has been reached in the institution of the Eucharist. Jesus spent only about thirty-three years upon this earth, and He confined Himself within the narrow limits of Palestine. Although He disdained human honors and wealth, as a man, He towered far above His contemporaries. They could disagree with Him; they could hurl their hatred at Him; nonetheless, they were obliged to recognize the ascendency of His authority.

But in the Eucharist, that sovereign charm which was an irradiation of His Godhead disappears. Only the semblance of bread remains, a semblance that has not the least vestige of form or beauty. Our God, our Almighty God, is entire in a Host so thin, so light that the breath of a baby could blow it away. He is entire in every fragment that at times, by accident, the priest lets fall upon the paten. As palaces, He has churches, some of which are poor, miserable, scarcely decent. And there He reigns, this King of kings, for days, for years, for centuries. Faithful to His promise, He will be with us until the end of all ages.[89] As though to make sure that His enemies can strike anywhere, He multiplies His presence. Wherever a

[89] Matt. 28:20.

priest summons Him, the heavens are opened, and lo, He comes.

"But it is sheer folly," one will say, "thus to abdicate His dignity, thus to take the form of a small piece of bread to be eaten by vile, frivolous, and sinful creatures." Such was somehow the arguing of the hearers of Jesus when, in the synagogue of Capharnaum, He announced the future institution of the Eucharist. "This saying is hard," they said, "and who can hear it?"[90] This saying is hard! Yes, it is, to those who belittle the Almighty. According to them, God should love us moderately, reasonably, measurably. They forget that God never stops halfway. According to the word of St. John, He loves "unto the end,"[91] that is to say, to a climax, to a paroxysm of love. "The folly of the Cross":[92] this has been said of the divine act of love on Golgotha. "The folly of the altar": this could be said of the summits of divine love as exemplified on the first Holy Thursday in the Upper Room of Jerusalem, and since then on every altar of Christendom.

God longs deeply for your love

Since God so loves us, no wonder He desires to be loved by us. Fatherly love is most unselfish. For all this, when a father has poured his whole kindness upon his children, he is entitled to some return. Nature and logic dictate and demand the fulfillment of such duty. Add to this that, for God, the desire to be loved is also the will to make us happy. He has fashioned

[90] John 6:61 (RSV = John 6:60).
[91] John 13:1.
[92] Cf. 1 Cor. 1:18.

us for Himself; He is our end, our perfection, our bliss. The hope to possess Him someday is the only true joy. In commanding us to love Him, God therefore commands us to be happy. If He imposes this obligation, it is for His glory, and it is also for our own interest.

This desire to be loved appears most conspicuously in the soul of Jesus. It is true that He does not say to His disciples: "Love me." He forgets Himself; He thinks only of His Father's glory. But all His words and deeds lead us to see the constant craving to touch our heart.

It is to conquer our love that He has performed His miracles. In them the part of compassion is as great as His desire to prove His divine mission. They are not mere wonders, done to awaken surprise and admiration; they are alleviations of human misery. And why has He willed to experience all our trials and be acquainted with our fragility and infirmities — childhood, poverty, temptation, death? It was so that we might have to give Him something, at least our sympathy. Having fashioned our heart, He knew that our affections grow, not according to the way we receive, but according to the way we give.

Once more, see His last meeting with St. Peter. He takes him aside and three times asks him with increasing insistence: "Simon, son of John, lovest thou me?"[93] A surprising question. He is about to return to His Father, but first He wants to know whether He is loved by one human being.

Who would not wonder at the condescension of our God? He is sovereignly great; compared with Him, we are nothing;

[93] John 21:15, 16, 17.

and on such nothingness He vouchsafes to cast His eyes. He is perfectly happy in Heaven; He owns the universe; and He coaxes us as though we could add something to His bliss. He stoops so low as to beg our love. If at least we had all the goodness that is consistent with our earthly condition! If our will were ever conformed to the divine will! But to the misery of his nature man adds the misery of sin. How is it, then, that in spite of His hatred for evil, God so pursues us and prizes our friendship so deeply?

The intensity of God's love explains what may perhaps be called His susceptibility. It has been rightly said that to love a friend is to give him the power to hurt us and to take from him the right to do so. If a stranger is impolite to us, we scarcely mind it. But one unkind word from a friend wounds us cruelly. We cannot help saying, "What have I done to him? I did not deserve this."

Now, God has so loved the world, He is so thirsty for our love, that He is offended by our least faults. He knows them all and forgets none of them. "Every idle word that men shall speak they shall render an account in the Day of Judgment,"[94] the Gospel tells us. An alarming prospect this is, when we remember that even "the just man shall fall seven times."[95] How often we are neglectful in God's service! How often we fail to perform our duty! And we shall atone for all that!

But here comes the counterpart: God is aware of our least act of irreverence to Him, but also of our feeblest effort to please Him. He is thankful that we have resisted that desire,

[94] Matt. 12:36.
[95] Prov. 24:16.

repulsed that distraction, and have not said that slanderous word by which we were tempted to sin. Whosoever shall give a cup of water in His name shall not lose his reward.[96] How comforting is such a promise!

Whatever our defects and our weaknesses may be, surely we have good will. It is for God that we labor. Now and then, it is true, we forget Him; but after fugitive wanderings, our thought ever returns to Him, like the magnetic needle to the pole. Since our intention is right, all our good works, all our pains, and even our temptations are for us occasions of merit. Every day, we heap up treasures in Heaven; we add to our capital. And if we die in the state of grace, we shall find a fortune for all eternity.

God demands much from laymen, but much more from those whom He calls to higher perfection and on whom He has especially lavished His grace. It is for this reason that He is especially sensitive to the sins of priests and religious. St. Teresa in her autobiography tells us that, should she happen to become remiss in her piety (was it ever so little), Christ never failed to tell her that He took notice of it.

For the same reason, because they know God's severity, the saints have only contempt for themselves. Pure as their lives are, they look upon themselves as great sinners, worthy of everlasting chastisements. Exaggerated language? Affected humility? No, indeed; the saints are sincere. They are aware of their special privileges. God loves them and purifies them of their least imperfections so that He may love them still more. Thus, He harasses them and leads them toward the heights.

[96] Matt. 10:42.

The saints are conscious of this divine solicitation, and seeing how far they are from what God wants them to be, they tremble and say, "Lord, shall I ever be able to satisfy Thee?"

‿

God is to be loved above all creation

"The Lord is a jealous God,"[97] we read in the Scriptures. This is another characteristic of divine love. God cannot abdicate His rights. We are His absolute property. He is supreme perfection. Created beauty pales before His splendor, as a star before the morning sun. Finite we are, but His infinitely. To the first place in our heart He has a sacred right that cannot be taken from Him.

He wants, therefore, to be loved above all things, but not exclusively. A heart dried and narrow is no offering worthy of Him. If there is a commandment that obliges us to love God, there is another that obliges us to love our neighbor.[98] But we must love Him "according to order,"[99] as He wills to be loved, and not more than He wills. Any illegitimate or excessive affection is an outrage to divine Majesty.

Jealousy is a passion that none dares avow; it is a vile, wicked feeling that ripens sometimes into madness. Needless to say, divine jealousy is pure and holy. Rightly considered, it is one form of infinite goodness. God knows that our heart is restless and storm-tossed until it is anchored in Him. When, therefore, we stubbornly seek for happiness in creatures, He deplores our folly and is indignant at it. "My people have done

---

[97] Nah. 1:2.
[98] Matt. 22:37, 39.
[99] 1 Cor. 14:40.

two evils. They have forsaken me, the fountain of living water, and have digged to themselves cisterns, broken cisterns that can hold no water."[100] These rebukes that God addressed to Israel are applicable also to those inconsistent Christians who daily tell Him, "My God, I love Thee above all things" and daily prefer anything to Him.

⸎

God's love helps you understand His justice

God's infinite love again helps us understand the rigor of His justice.

Quite well I know that during the present life, God hates no one. Since He obliges us to forgive, not only once, but seventy times seven times,[101] that is to say, indefinitely, He obliges Himself to the same law. According to the expression of the psalmist, a contrite and humble heart He will not despise.[102] Except the sin against the Holy Spirit,[103] all sins can be forgiven before death.

But the time for mercy must have an end. When, until the last moment, a man refuses God's grace, when he dies repulsing the hand extended to save him, what will the sovereign Judge do? Is He not compelled to say to such an obstinate sinner, "You have selected your own fate. You have cast me away. I cast you away"? And where will he go, that unfortunate? He will go far from God, who is light, joy, and life, to darkness, sorrow, and death eternal!

---

[100] Jer. 2:13.
[101] Matt. 18:21.
[102] Ps. 50:19 (RSV = Ps. 51:17).
[103] Cf. Matt. 12:32; Mark 3:29; Luke 12:10.

⤳

God sends His trials delicately

To understand how God governs us, consider His attributes and also the object of His care.

We have said before that man is weakness itself. Because he is limited in his knowledge, the future is to him a mystery. He is only a vapor that the least wind dissipates. His life lasts the time that a match flickers. A reed he is, as Pascal says, but a reed that can think and suffer; a reed that has the power to serve the designs of God or to combat them. Man's salvation is partly his own work.

Let us note also that there is a great variety in the works of God — in man still more than in nature. Each individual has his own mark, his own physiognomy. Wisdom demands that such diversity be reckoned with, and God proceeds wisely in accordance with it — so many souls, so many methods.

See how delicately God sends His trials. He proportions them to our strength — to great souls, heavy burdens. The size of our cross depends on our stature.

Can we believe that coming events cast their shadows before? No, nor can we believe that the sunset of life gives us mystical lore.[104] But without falling into superstition, we may think that God, so good and wise, forewarns and forearms us before imposing upon us burdens that crush. He always proceeds gradually. "First the blade, then the ear, afterward the full corn in the ear."[105] He trains and prepares us, and makes us, as it were, enter a novitiate of suffering.

---

[104] Cf. Thomas Campbell, "Lochiel's Warning."
[105] Mark 4:28.

It has often been noticed that God followed a similar method in the moral education of mankind. While His own chosen people were still wrapped in the swaddling clothes of the Mosaic law, He did not demand from them any self-renunciation. It is by the allurement of earthly bliss that He led them to the practice of virtue. "Blessed is the man that feareth the Lord: he shall delight exceedingly in His commandments. His seed shall be mighty upon earth. The generation of the righteous shall be blessed. Glory and wealth shall be in his house. I have been young, and now I am old; and I have not seen the just forsaken, nor his seed seeking bread."[106]

How different is the language of the divine Master! "Amen, I say to you, that you shall lament and weep, but the world shall rejoice; and you shall be made sorrowful, but your sorrow shall be turned into joy."[107] In passing from the Old Testament to the Gospel, it seems that we pass from one world to another. Whence comes this difference, or rather, this opposition? It comes from the fact that, in the interval, humanity had grown stronger. Invigorated by the examples and the grace of Christ, it possessed a new ideal, a larger and loftier ideal. The Jews who did not accept Jesus believed that the law of Moses was perfect and final; they did not understand that a man's clothes must fit his size, and that the chrysalis must turn into a winged butterfly.

God, who prepares us from afar for our great trials, takes care also to assuage them. There are compromises and counterpoises in His way of governing us. To the intoxication of

---

[106] Ps. 111:1-3, 36:25 (RSV = Ps. 112:1-3, 37:25).
[107] John 16:20.

success He opposes bitter deceptions. On the other hand, He comforts those whom He hurts. By such blending of good and evil, He maintains us in equilibrium and keeps us both from presumption and from despair.

In combining the laws of nature, God has foreseen relief to our sorrows — sleep, for instance, that care-charmer that slides into our souls and is the consoler of us all. "He giveth His beloved sleep."[108] During the night, sorrows dissolve themselves and lose their bitterness. It is also often noticed that a pain never increases in proportion to its causes. Having reached a certain degree, it remains stationary. A climax has arrived. When people are very ill, they become indifferent to everything except their health. All other anxieties are gone. Again, in the midst of trials, the soul hardens itself and bears up against misfortune — so much so as to become insensitive to suffering.

Besides such natural helps, common to all, God's Providence sends special supernatural consolations. At times, it is some good news or some pleasant visitor, and this single dewdrop of joy is enough to fill the chalice of our heart. Witness St. Paul: "I am filled with comfort: I exceedingly abound with joy in all our tribulation. For also, when we were come into Macedonia, our flesh had no rest: we suffered all tribulation — combats without, fears within. But God, who comforteth the humble, comforted us by the coming of Titus."[109]

Plentiful and continuous are those heavenly consolations. Not one day passes without being enlivened by a ray of the

---

[108] Cf. Ps. 126:2 (RSV = Ps. 127:2).
[109] 2 Cor. 7:4-6.

sun. God never loses sight of us and sends us frequent messages. And He always proportions the consolation to the trial.

Restless was the life of St. Paul as described in his second letter to the Corinthians. Persecutions, betrayals, shipwrecks, deceptions, temptations, infirmities — he knew all forms of human suffering. And yet, far from displaying dejection or sadness, his letters vibrate with the enthusiasm of happiness.

Does this mean that mystical souls are extremists? No, but even in the midst of distress, they enjoy God's consolation. Their interior life is like a stormy sky toward which ascends the silvery sound of the *Angelus;* while the thunder roars and trees are shaken, the bell rings, soft and calm.[110] Distinct as they are, the two voices are heard. Yes, the soul may stay at peace when the heart is bleeding.

Thus it is that God deals with those whom He tries, suavely and strongly. He does not spare them; He cuts them to the quick. But how gently He binds the wounds He has inflicted!

"Verily," says Isaiah, "Thou art a hidden God."[111] God is a hidden God, not only in this sense that He is invisible by nature, but because, aware of our weakness and respectful of our liberty, He keeps us ignorant of His gifts, His operations, His designs, and, consequently, our destiny.

༺

God reveals to you only what you need to know

If we knew the gifts of God, if we were conscious of the operations of His grace, and especially if we were sure of our

---

[110] Church bells are often rung in the morning, at noon, and in the evening to call the faithful to pray the *Angelus* prayer.

[111] Isa. 45:15.

salvation, our joy would be great, but it would be dangerous also! How strong the temptation to be presumptuous and slothful would be! Why strive to go forward, since an infinite power uplifts us and drives us irresistibly? Let us rest in our boat on the divine ocean.

To inspire in us a salutary fear, and to keep us on the alert, God leaves us in relative ignorance.

God warms us with His peace and joy. But his ways of acting remain hidden. When, purified and forgiven, we leave the tribunal of Penance, we cannot notice the passage from the state of sin to the state of grace. There has been no commotion whatever. Faith alone tells us of the change within us. Likewise, when we receive Holy Communion, we are not conscious of the increase of moral energy that is communicated to us. God ever acts discreetly and sanctifies us silently.

It is usually long after their occurrence that we notice the intervention of God's Providence in the external events of our life. When Joseph was sold by his brethren, unjustly accused, and sent to prison, he could have thought he was abandoned by God. All appearances were against him. If his faith had not been so fervent, his would have been the dark pessimism of those who cry out, "Virtue has not paid me." God, however, was with him, and prepared him for his great mission. Later on, when Benjamin was arrested by the servants of Joseph, because their master's silver cup was found in his sack of corn, he also could have thought that he was abandoned by God. But what he took for a misfortune was only a contrivance inspired by brotherly love, and really a blessing in disguise.[112]

[112] Cf. Gen. 44:12 ff.

Thus, when trial comes, we see at first only the troubles it involves; but by and by, recognizing how beneficent it has been, we have to salute it as one of God's harbingers.

The past is fraught with divineness. So is the present, but unless we have the spirit of faith, it first appears under its natural aspect, which most often is commonplace and unpleasant. It is only after it has disappeared that it transfigures itself in our memory, and the divine side of it is revealed. For instance, on the mountain, Moses perceived the glory of Jehovah only when it departed;[113] the disciples at Emmaus recognized their companion only after His visible form had disappeared.[114]

God hides His designs and His ways of acting. It must be admitted that He is not bound to reveal them to us. No general ever feels obliged to explain to all his soldiers his plan of campaign. He gives orders, and in executing them, each unit collaborates with the design of the chief. Even so, God signifies His will day by day, hour by hour. What His projects are we do not always know.

When he willed to make Abraham the father of a great nation, He said to him, "Go forth out of thy country, and from thy kindred, and come into the land which I shall show thee."[115] Where that land was Abraham was not told, but he went out as the Lord had commanded him, and, in time, he received new directions. The patriarch was as discreet with his son as God had been with him. On the slopes of Mount Moriah, with wood on his shoulders, Isaac said to his father,

[113] Exod. 33:18-23.
[114] Luke 24:31.
[115] Gen. 12:1.

"Behold, fire and wood. Where is the victim for the holocaust?" And Abraham answered, "God will provide Himself a victim, my son."[116]

When Saul fell to the ground on his way to Damascus, the Lord said to him, "Arise, and go into the city, and there it shall be told thee what thou must do."[117] Saul obeyed, and three days later, Ananias came to instruct him.

Many similar events can be found in the lives of the saints. John Baptist de la Salle,[118] when a canon of the Rheims Cathedral, was interested in school work, but from on high and from afar, as it were. Soon, however, he saw that, to train children in virtue and piety, it was necessary to have teachers who were earnest, devoted to their task, and profoundly impregnated with the Christian spirit. The idea came to him to gather a few of them into his home. He started reluctantly, for, imbued with the prejudices of his time, he looked upon a schoolteacher as less than a valet. But soon the truth imposed itself with the force of evidence: to be efficacious, a sermon must be put into practice. He took a heroic resolution; he resigned his charge, gave away his patrimony, adopted the garb of his Brothers, and followed their rule. Thus, progressively, God manifested His designs to him and, as He demanded a new sacrifice, gave him also the grace to offer it.

This is God's method. When we place ourselves into His hands, we do not know exactly to what we engage ourselves.

---

[116] Gen. 22:7-8.

[117] Acts 9:6.

[118] St. John Baptist de la Salle (1651-1719), founder of the Institute of the Brothers of Christian Schools.

So much the better! For a premature revelation, perhaps, would cause us too much fear.

☙

God's purposes are often hidden

The same discretion is always found in God's way of governing us. It is true that He always hears our prayers, but He does not necessarily hear them in the same sense as we do. To the inquiry of the Apostles — "Wilt Thou at this time restore again the kingdom of Israel?" — our Lord replied, "It is not for you to know the times which the Father hath put in His own power."[119]

Until the last day, they kept their visionary hope, and so their disillusionment was bitter when Jesus was arrested, condemned, and crucified — for the King of Israel, a gibbet as a throne, a crown of thorns as a diadem! And in their confusion, the disciples had no thought that Jesus, dying to save the world, was more beautiful on His Cross than He would have been on a golden throne studded with jewels. As to the Apostles, they have had more influence and fame than if, their puny ambition being satisfied, they had become rulers in the little kingdom of Israel.

We may admit that God does not always hear our prayers literally, but He interprets our desires in a sense more suitable to our dignity and to His secret designs.

It may also be observed that sometimes God awakens within us desires that He does not intend to satisfy. Because our plans have not been carried out, we think we have wasted our time. By no means. God has turned to account those deeds

---

[119] Acts 1:6-7.

which we have performed and has used them for a purpose
that someday He will reveal.

To reconquer Jerusalem, St. Louis attempted two crusades
that, humanly speaking, were lamentable failures. Defeats, ep-
idemics, captivity, shipwrecks — no calamity was spared his
army. And yet the pious king, when in agony near the walls of
Tunis, would say with confidence, "We shall reach Jerusalem."
A mysterious and touching word this is. St. Louis died without
having realized his dream. Not even from afar did he see the
earthly Jerusalem. But he conquered the other, the more beautiful one. His work was no failure — far from it, since it devel-
oped his courage and increased his merits. And who knows
whether the noble example of humility, patience, and generosity that he gave to the world has not been more useful to the
Church than the conquest of the Holy Lands?

Yet more unfathomable are God's designs over nations.
With men and events, He fashions a mosaic, the beauty of
which we can grasp only when it is finished. When we study
history, we admire the profound wisdom with which He has
made the best of everything, even persecutions, schisms, and
heresies, for the extension of His reign. In the midst of darkness, the witnesses of those catastrophes are tempted to say
that all is lost. They are mistaken, for over the waters of the
flood floats an ark that carries the seed and hope of salvation.
It is true that the ark cannot always be seen. Vainly do they
scrutinize the sky to see whether a savior is coming. So grave
seems the situation that despair sets in. But God is there. He
watches the course of events, and at the right moment, He
Himself intervenes and gives to the problem a solution as simple as unexpected.

God's secret is not ours. He never permits the forecasting of the future. When we abandon ourselves to His leadership, it seems that we navigate on a writhing river flowing between high banks. There is no horizon; we are, as it were, on a lake that has no outlet. But the current draws us, and lo, there is a new winding. Thus is life: scarcely are we out of a difficulty than another appears, and we do not see how we shall succeed in extricating ourselves from it.

God hides our earthly future. He also hides our eternal future. Are our names written on the book of life? God alone knows and will keep His secret until our last breath. Such silence is prudent, for if we were assured of our salvation, what danger of presumption; and if we were sure of our perdition, what despair!

⌒

God respects your liberty

Compassionate with our weakness, God respects also our liberty. He wills to raise us to the dignity of our station, make us partakers, in a certain measure, of His creative power and independence. It is for this reason that He carefully veils the splendors of His glory and speaks so discreetly. A notorious lecturer once sputtered these blasphemous words in a public hall: "If God appeared to us here in visible form, our duty would be to refuse Him obedience and to tell Him, 'We are our own masters and do not need You.'" The speaker was no thinker, and never had weighed the meaning of the word *infinite*.

So majestic is God that if we could have a glimpse of Him, we would be dazzled and bewildered. We would be no more able to resist Him than a drop of water is able to resist the current that carries it away. In our actual state of weakness, the visible presence of God would paralyze our liberty. Therefore, He conceals Himself from our eyes, as a master who, to give self-conduct to His pupils, withdraws for a while and leaves them to the safeguard of their conscience.

It is for the same reason that the Son of God became a man in the conditions that we know. Jesus is incomparable in the order of charity. But He does not rely on our human power. Few, very few, acknowledge Him as He is. His is a veiled splendor, bright enough to attract sincere minds, obscure enough to tranquilize the minds of those who refuse to see Him.

God has not changed. He is eternally active, but behind a cloud. At times, the cloud flickers, and we have a glimpse of the divine deeds. The holy of holies is not empty.[120] God is never far from us. Many, however, will not see Him or understand Him! To them any fact looked upon as miraculous has a natural cause that science someday will discover. And comforted by such pretext, they strengthen themselves in their unbelief. Assent to religious truths is a free act, inspired by love as well as by evidence. What would be the merit of faith if our dogmas could be demonstrated like geometrical theorems?

☞

God desires your cooperation

Again, to let our activity have its own course, instead of pointing out the road we must take, God makes us search for it. In a general manner, His will is clearly signified by the Ten Commandments, by necessity, and by the orders of our superiors. But how many times is it almost as difficult to know one's

[120] Heb. 9:3 ff.

duty as to fulfill it! How many cases of conscience are so intricate as to seem insoluble! Their adjustment demands not only much reflection and shrewdness, but also absolute impartiality. Duty's voice is heard only if one silences interest and passion.

The same discretion is required to hear the calls of God. "Behold, I stand at the gate and knock," He says. "If any man shall hear my voice and open to me the door, I will come in to him and will sup with him, and he with me."[121] He enters the home of our heart only if we answer His call. Three times He called Samuel, and He entrusted a mission to him only after the child had answered, "Speak, Lord, for Thy servant heareth."[122] Thus God manifests a man's vocation. He proposes it without imposing it. What His views are He does not clearly indicate. He seems to wait for a step or a word on our part, a less incomplete surrender, or at least a movement of generosity.

Admirable also is the manner in which God measures His grace. If He gave it too abundantly, our will would be fatally drawn and driven to do good; but then we could not have any more merit in observing the law than the planets have in traveling over their orbits. Coercion would supplant action. Divine grace would be like those electric currents which, having too much energy, burn the fuse and give no light.

God, therefore, dispenses His grace not with parsimony, but with wisdom. He helps us to walk; He does not carry us. His grace, although sufficient in itself, becomes efficacious only with the concurrence of our will.

---

[121] Apoc. 3:20 (RSV = Rev. 3:20).
[122] 1 Kings 3:10 (RSV = 1 Sam. 3:10).

Does this mean that in that wondrous cooperation of the infinitely great with the infinitely small, the leadership is on our side? No, indeed. Without any violence, God ever leads us where He wills. He has always the last word in all human affairs. While we steer our ship, heedful of the wind and the reefs and the rocks, He, the invisible Pilot, remains near us and, when He deems it useful, handles the helm in person.

⌒

God's Providence adapts itself to you

Reckoning both with our weakness and our dignity, God's Providence adapts itself to mankind in general and to each human being in particular.

This fact has been denied by Malebranche and several other philosophers. According to them, God is the only Cause absolutely efficient. Without Him, there are only occasional causes. It is God who gives us light and heat — not the sun; the ray that strikes our retina is only the occasion provoking the divine intervention. God conforms Himself to the general laws that He has enacted.

But this is a doctrine that happily is denied by reason, Tradition, and Holy Scripture. The truth is that God takes particular care of each one of us, as we saw earlier. We need only open the Gospels to see how flexibly, as it were, the divine Master acts or speaks according to the circumstances and the character of persons and places. To the rich young man who, He knows, is attached to his great possessions, He promises a treasure in Heaven.[123] To fishermen who have known what a good catch is and have known also what the pangs of hunger

[123] Matt. 19:21.

are, He says, "Come ye after me, and I will make you to be fish-
ers of men. . . . And I dispose to you a kingdom, that you may
eat and drink at my table, in my kingdom."[124] To the paralytic
at Bethsaida who had been thirty-eight years under his infirmity, He inspires fear: "Behold, thou art made whole: sin no
more, lest some worse thing happen to thee."[125] He confounds
the learned Nicodemus in revealing to him a great mystery,
and seeing him astonished, He asks this question: "Art thou a
master in Israel, and knowest not these things?"[126] Thus Jesus
modifies His manner according to his audience. He is all to all
to bring them all to truth.

God's Providence is led by the same principle. Far from being uniform, it acts according to the circumstances of time and
persons. Vocation, for instance, is determined by individual
aptitudes, or, to speak more exactly, those aptitudes have been
imparted in view of a vocation. God fashions those whom He
calls. He prepares them from their mother's womb.

To reach sinners and bring them back to Him, He turns to
account the things to which they are partial. Huysmans,[127]
who had an artistic temperament, was attracted by the beauty
of cathedrals and the charm of Liturgy. Brunetiere was so fond
of Bossuet that at last he adopted his Faith. One man sees in
the Catholic Church a principle of good order, a great school
of respect, and the strongest of all social supports. Another is
drawn by the tenderness of the Gospels, the security, the

[124] Matt. 4:19; Luke 22:29-30.

[125] John 5:14.

[126] John 3:10.

[127] Joris Karl Huysmans (1848-1907), French Catholic novelist.

consolation, and the moral energy that arise from religious beliefs. Christianity presents itself to each individual under the aspect that best answers his aspirations. Ever varied is the drama of conversions. Each convert has his own personal motives. All roads lead to Rome.

As water takes the form of the vase that contains it, divine grace varies according to the souls into which it enters. If Malebranche has not perceived such truth, it is because he has carried into extremes his principle that God ever acts in the simplest way.

It is true that God never does anything useless and always avoids complexity. His is always the shortest way, and His aims frequently reach several ends. For instance, in punishing the guilty, He leads them to repentance, He vindicates His rights that have been violated, and He gives to all a salutary lesson. He satisfies His justice, wisdom, and goodness. In order that His intervening may be not too apparent, He produces great effects through little causes. He uses ignorance to confound human wisdom, and human weakness to crush human strength; witnesses of this are the Apostles, Judith, and Joan of Arc. But what hides Him from the eyes of the world is precisely what manifests Him to the eyes of the faithful, for the worker proves himself the more clever when the tool he handles is not proportionate to its end. "This day," David said to Goliath, "all the earth shall know that there is a God in Israel. And all this assembly shall know that the Lord saveth not with sword and spear; for it is His battle, and He will deliver thee into our hands."[128]

---

[128] 1 Kings 17:46-47 (RSV = 1 Sam. 17:46-47).

In fact, what we notice first in the divine deeds is not their simplicity, but their variety and complexity. God changes His tactics according to the souls He wishes to conquer. No two of them are endowed with the same aptitudes; no two of them are led along the same road; no two of them are expected to give the same service. The true Light, which enlightens every man coming into this world, infinitely varies the intensity and the color of its rays. Hence, the extreme prudence that spiritual directors must have; they have to be careful before making a decision, lest they thwart the designs of God.

What makes more complex the task of Divine Providence is the fact of our liberty. We are tied to the throne of God by a chain that holds us without enslaving us. It is true that in His struggle with human liberty, God at times seems vanquished. His work is ruined through our faults; but without losing any time, He begins to reconstruct it on another plan, larger and more beautiful. It is thus that, after the sin of our first parents, He has re-established humanity. And who will not see that He has displayed more than wisdom and love in the work of Redemption than in the work of Creation?

God's ways are sometimes beyond your understanding

Hitherto we have seen the ways of God's Providence that can be understood. But there are others that tower above our reason. And no wonder. When we deal with divinity, we collide with mystery.

We have said that vocation supposes certain aptitudes and that God carefully prepares those He calls to religious or priestly life. Does this mean that He always selects those who are most apt? No. He sorts them, but He does not necessarily choose those who are most intelligent, or even most pious. He leaves in the world, or prematurely recalls to Himself, young men who, according to all appearances, would have been remarkable priests. What is His reason in doing so? We do not know. We cannot know.

It is cause for still more wonder that, after having lengthily prepared an apostolic worker, God stops him when his activity is most intense and fruitful. St. Francis Xavier[129] was raised to the priesthood when about thirty years old, and he died fifteen years later, near the coast of China, which he wished to conquer. If that extraordinary man had lived twenty years more, how many new provinces he would have annexed to the Church! He was taken away before he had given his full measure, and like many others, he had to leave his plough in the middle of the field.

God proceeds in the order of grace as in the order of nature. In the formation of individuals, He displays wonderful patience and wisdom, but these masterpieces fashioned with so much artistry He breaks as things of no value. The fallen oak once covered with its vast branches a whole stretch of sky. It was straight, robust, and magnificent. A clap of thunder crushed it, and the work of centuries was destroyed in a moment.

The history of conversions raises problems no less insoluble. Christ had two fellow sufferers near Him on Calvary. Both were probably guilty in the same degree. One, however, died as a reprobate; the other saw the gates of Heaven ajar. Why this difference? Why did God choose Jacob and reject Esau? We

---

[129] St. Francis Xavier (1506-1552), missionary to the East Indies and to Japan.

read in the Gospel, "Two women shall be grinding at the mill; one shall be taken, and one shall be left."[130] Why this one rather than the other? We know not.

A chaplain who, during the Great War, was a genuine conqueror of souls, has acknowledged, not without surprise, that those more easily moved by divine grace were not always those who seemed to be the best or the most honest. Rather were they those who had no appearance of sanctity. Unexpected resources, a predisposition to believe, a craving for virtue, and a sincere generosity were found in them. They were the chaplain's "dear rascals." After a disorderly life, many of them had an edifying death. Where was the merit of their conversion? Who can tell?

If we deal with the call to salvation or with final perseverance, the problem is still more obscure. It is certain that God wills the salvation of all men. It also is certain that, being sovereignly good and wise, He will not reject forever the heretics who are in good faith or the pagans who have always obeyed the voice of their conscience. But, outside of Christianity, are such faithful observers of the natural law in any great number?

If, with all the helps lavished on us, it is still not an easy task to triumph over all temptations, what of those who are less favored than we are? Their passions, not cooled by Baptism, have more force and fury. Their will, deprived of the sacramental strength, is still more frail and inconstant than ours. Imagine a man born of faithless parents who has been taught only a vague morality with no obligation nor sanction. What has he to counterbalance the urge of his instinct? And what

[130] Matt. 24:41.

shall we say of that numberless multitude of men who, having lived before Christ, have not known His teaching and examples? What shall we say of those prehistoric men whose culture and ethics were almost nonexistent? What moral support could they find in their coarse superstitions?

Our condition is incomparably better. We have much more facility for our salvation. What has been the cause of such a privilege? It is a gratuitous favor from Him who said, "I will have mercy on whom I will, and I will be merciful to whom it shall please me."[131] He has called us; He has justified us by Baptism and Penance. May He save us!

There is, therefore, a predestination that is not determined in all cases by the prevision of merits. How many children die after Baptism without having done anything to gain Heaven! Why does God take some and leave the others? Because such has been His good pleasure. In the present state of our knowledge, we cannot find and we cannot seek other reasons.

If we consider things merely from a human viewpoint, the distribution of consolations and trials also appears capricious and inconstant.

In some periods of our life, we have a very clear and comforting impression that we are in the hands of God's Providence. Everything smiles at us. We see our whole life. A star shines before us and guides our march. But all of a sudden comes an eclipse, and we are like the Magi, surprised, misled, and asking our way.

Is such a trial a punishment for our sins? It seems so, but the greatest saints, those who never refuse anything to God, know

[131] Exod. 33:19.

also such alternatives of fervor and aridity, spiritual sweetness and desolation. It is not given us to prevent such vicissitudes: "The Spirit breatheth where He will, and thou hearest His voice, but thou knowest not whence He cometh and whither He goeth."[132] Divine activity is like the ebb and flow of the ocean; it has regular and irregular movements that surprise us. It is like the sun, which shines and suddenly stops shining.

God's reasons for sending afflictions are seldom clear to us. Witnesses of the long and cruel agony of a little child, we ask almost unconsciously, "What has he done to deserve such pain? Of what use are sufferings that are neither chastisement nor a remedy?"

Such problems would be full of anguish, if we did not know that this present life is only a passage, a beginning that shall lead to eternity.

⌒

God's view sees all

We must remember also that God's viewpoint is not the same as ours. Each of us is inclined to think of nothing but self. The best of us, the most generous, forget themselves to take interest in their family, their country, and their Church. But God's thoughts are incomparably loftier and larger. He contemplates His whole immense empire, which embraces not only humanity, but also the numberless phalanxes of angels. Center of the universe, He subordinates everything to Himself; it is His right, His essential and inalienable right. As He is wisdom and goodness, He knows how to coordinate the good of individuals with the interests of His glory. He neglects none

---

[132] John 3:8.

of the works of His hands, not even a flower or a blade of grass. It is nonetheless true that, to understand His method of government, it would be necessary to see things as He sees them. And this is impossible.

Why, then, disturb ourselves with puzzles that we cannot solve? Our knowledge is limited. The genesis of things is lost in impenetrable depths. The threads that lead men and events cross each other and are inextricably entangled, but their extremities are in the hand of God. If one day, as it is our firm hope, we are reunited to our principle, ours will be the right coin of vantage, and everything will be clear. We will see that what is defective in one way is useful in another way. Then we shall hear the whole concert, not only a few notes; and the dissonances will melt into the harmony of the whole.

⁀

God's mystery leads the soul to adoration
While expecting the hour of such revelation, let us not be ruffled by the fact that we are now facing a mystery. Mystery best reveals divine infinitude. It invites us to adore what we cannot understand. When we have justified God's Providence, and when we have had a glimpse of His designs and methods, a spark of joy illuminates our soul. It is as though a ray of divine glory had appeared before us. And yet the problems that are given to us to solve are only the simplest. The others will lead us deeper into the knowledge of God, and their difficulty will make us feel how puny is our reason and how infinite its object. The more incomprehensible is God the greater He appears. The beauty of creatures is necessarily limited; the beauty of God consists in its very infinity.

Chapter Four

*Providence calls
for your response*

Thus far, we have seen that God takes care of His creatures, all of them in general and each of them in particular; we have seen the means He uses and the rules He follows in His government. It remains to consider our duties toward God's Providence and the habitual feelings of those who trust in Him.

Our duties may be summed up in three words: understanding, obedience, and gratitude.

☙

To appreciate Providence, you must consider God's view

When we have to live with a certain person, our first care is to study his manners, his tastes, and his habits, so that we may accommodate ourselves to his character, understand him, and never hurt him. Now, between God and man, there are necessary and permanent dealings. It is in Him that we live and move and have our being.[133] He is the soul of our soul. Whether or not we have the consciousness of His presence, He always acts around us and in us. It behooves us, therefore, to know His designs and His ways of acting; if not, we risk marching on the wrong side, ill-advisedly, imprudently, and illogically.

[133] Cf. Acts 17:28.

The general design of God is to save us — that is to say, to have us share His eternal joy. If He sees that the goods of this world are an obstacle to our salvation, He does not hesitate to take them away from us. In doing so, He proves His wisdom and mercy. He thwarts us because He loves us. But to realize that, we must enter into His own views and consider all things from the aspect of eternity. Those who see only the present life, and in this present life only pleasure and well-being, are indignant when suffering is mentioned as good. "The natural man perceiveth not these things that are of the Spirit of God."[134] Not seeing the secret reason of the trial, they execrate the hand that strikes them, as tiny children who scream when their mother washes them or dresses their wounds.

Another source of misunderstanding between God and man is that some of us want to be the very center of everything. If we do not go so far as to say, "I am, and there is none beside me," we act as if it was our conviction. We think merely of advancing ourselves, without any care for, and even to the detriment of, our associates. Nothing is more absurd, nothing more hideous than such unconscious egocentrism. We are only an insignificant part of the universe. If a man lives only for himself and wants to profit by the labor of others, he is unjust, for an individual must be subordinate to society; he is illogical also, for he is not self-sufficient and can live only with society.

Not less unreasonable are those egotists who, careless of the general good, would violate divine and human laws to gain enjoyment. They are not in order, for a member's will must be the whole body's will.

[134] Cf. 1 Cor. 2:14.

This is what Pascal has well expressed in his *Thoughts:* "When God created the heavens and the earth, which could feel no happiness in their own existence, it pleased Him to create also a race of beings who should feel this, and who should constitute a body of thinking members. All men are members of this body; and for their happiness, it was requisite that their individual will should be conformed to the general will by which the whole body is regulated.

"Yet it often happens that one man thinks himself an independent whole, and that, losing sight of the body with which he is associated, he believes that he depends only on himself, and wishes to be his own center, and his own circumference. But he finds himself in this state, like a member amputated from the body, and having in himself no principle of life, he only wanders and becomes more confused in the uncertainty of his own existence.

"But when at length a man begins rightly to know himself, he is, as it were, returned to his senses; he feels that he is not the body; he understands that he is only a member of the universal body, and that to be a member is to have no life, being, or motion, but the spirit of the body, and for the body; that a member separated from the body to which it belongs has only an expiring existence; and that he ought to love himself only for the sake of the body, or, rather, that he should love only the whole body, because in loving that, he loves himself, seeing that only in it, for it, and by it, has he any existence."

How simple and clear life would be if such thoughts were ours! Events throw us out of sorts because we consider them from our personal viewpoint. It is not only for us that God governs the world. Our little sphere is only an imperceptible part of the immense world that God has created. This is what we must not forget.

When the course of events is contrary to our provisions and desires, this is no reason to murmur against Divine Providence. Let us not imitate that fatuous and impertinent king of Castille, who, proud of his astronomical knowledge, could find many flaws in celestial mechanics. Ah, if God had only consulted him before creating the world! Such is human reason: as bold as it is blind, and ever unable to judge the works of God. God has his reasons, which our reason cannot always understand, but wisdom foresees them, and before the mystery where the Infinite hides Himself, we must bow as we do before the veils of the tabernacle.

꩜

God reveals His will in small ways

It is not enough to know the general design of God. He has particular plans for us. To permit us to accomplish our mission He has endowed us with certain talents, favored us with special graces, and led us in a fixed direction. How can we understand His action if we do not know what service He expects from us?

Not only does He call us to a state of life and entrust us with a mission, but He is precise in His instructions and dictates our duty day by day, hour by hour.

To listen to this divine voice is the great occupation of religious souls. Will their resolution please God? Such is their frequent query. They act in peace only if they are morally sure that the Master approves them.

When the Amalecites had invaded his city of refuge, David, through the priest Abiathar, consulted the Lord: "Shall we pursue after these robbers, and shall we overtake them or not?"[135] And only after having received a favorable answer did he decide to wage war. Thus do those act who have the true spirit of faith. When their duty is not clear, they say, like Saul on the way to Damascus, "Lord, what will Thou have me to do?"[136] God does not, of course, appear to them in a visible form, but He speaks through the voice of their conscience.

To preserve us from illusion, always easy in such cases, He has given us signs that help us to recognize His will. First, He gives us the divine law, natural or revealed; then the positive law, which is enacted by ecclesiastical or civil authority; also the commands of our superiors, the admonitions of spiritual directors, the examples of the saints, and, most of all, the examples of the divine Master. When in doubt, ask yourself what He would do, and almost always there will be light in your soul.

Events that do not depend on our will are also valuable indications. When, in spite of our efforts, our work has been a failure, this may be a sign that God willed to make us deserve success, but not reach it; success would not have been good for us, this time at least.

Events are also God's messengers in reviving the impression of a religious truth or in proposing the fulfillment of a task. A priest is invited to deliver a sermon, or to go on a sick call. It is God who asks him to work for His glory. Those whose faith is fervent frequently think of such providential indications. Thus, St. Paul tells us that he went to preach the Gospel

[135] Cf. 1 Kings 30:8 (RSV = 1 Sam. 30:8).
[136] Acts 9:6.

in Troas, because "a door was open to him in the Lord,"[137] that is to say, the Lord had offered him a propitious occasion.

⌒

You must be attentive to
manifestations of God's will

Such are the principal signs that manifest the will of God. All have not the same evidence nor the same value. Some are less apparent; some are doubtful and even suspicious. How shall we discriminate and appreciate them?

The first condition is that we must be watchful. Because He respects our liberty, God speaks in a low voice. His voice has the sound of faraway music. To tepid or sinful souls He speaks of their unfaithfulness; He calls them back to a better life, but how discreetly! To hear Him, both attention and recollection are necessary.

Such attention must be permanent, for He comes at any time. What Christ said of His second coming may be applied also to His daily visits: "Be you ready, for at what hour you think not, the Son of Man will come."[138] The true disciple of Christ is, therefore, always on the alert: he is like lookout men who from their observatory scan the horizon, attentive to the signals that may come from beacons or from semaphores.

Such signals are understood only by those who have been taught their meaning. One and all can see the movements of the antennae and the luminous projections, but their meaning is intelligible only to the few. So it is with providential events. They are usually minute facts that appear insignificant.

[137] 2 Cor. 2:12.
[138] Luke 12:40.

When St. Augustine heard his famous *"Tolle, lege,"* he could have said, "This is an accidental coincidence and nothing else." But moved by grace, he interpreted this incident, and he was saved. Following the example of this great Doctor, fervent Christians see all things with the eyes of faith; it is the only way to recognize God's guidance hidden under humble appearances.

Our Savior appeared to Mary of Magdala as a gardener, and He met the pilgrims of Emmaus as an unknown traveler.[139] In these our days, He visits us differently clad. A poor man knocks at our door; it is Christ who speaks and gives us the occasion to be charitable to Him. Someone calls on us; humanly speaking, it is only an incident pleasant or tedious, but which is quite different if we look upon it from a supernatural standpoint. This unexpected visitor is sent by God's Providence. Perhaps he will tell you words that will influence your whole life. Perhaps he will ask you, O good Samaritan, to pour in oil and wine on the wound of his soul,[140] and draw him out of the slough of despondency, scruple, or sin.

☞

*You must learn to discern
the voice of God*

We must learn also how to discern the voice of God. Not all events are portents. None of them, it is true, happen without God's will or permission, but it does not follow that they all bring special messages to us. Many of them do not concern us, and there is no need to try to find a meaning in them. Only

---

[139] Cf. John 20:15; Luke 24:15-16.
[140] Cf. Luke 10:33-34.

weak-minded people pay attention to signs and portents that are nothing but remnants of paganism.

The ancients were superstitious; the crash of thunder, the singing of birds — everything to them indicated the will of the gods. There was in Rome a college of sixteen priests supposedly endowed with augural knowledge whom the senate consulted before taking important steps. A stupid superstition this was.

God reveals Himself when and where it pleases Him to do so. No need to codify or foresee His acts. Humbly and obediently, let us walk in His presence, ready to notice the signs of His holy will.

*You must learn to distinguish between
your own inclinations and God's call*

We must learn also how to discern the voice of our own appetites and feelings.

Nothing is more deceptive than the movements of our sensitiveness. Here is a young novice who craves special mortifications. He thinks that such works of supererogation will purify his soul and bring him nearer to God. But it may be that he is led to them by a desire to make himself conspicuous and prove how strong he is. Perhaps also, unconsciously, he is played upon by the Devil; he will ruin his health and become a burden to his community.

We also run the risk of deceiving ourselves if, to determine our special vocation, we reckon only with the fact of its attractiveness. Usually a vocation manifests itself gradually, and, while the dawn is not yet the day, mistakes may occur concerning God's intentions.

Obsessed by a desire for perfection, St. John of the Cross,[141] then a Carmelite, thought of becoming a Carthusian; and he would have realized his project if he had not met Teresa of Avila at Medina del Campo. In his first talk with the saint, his aspirations toward a perfect life turned to the reforming of Carmel. He had found his way.

St. Teresa herself, scarcely seven years old, wished to go to the foreign missions. She had been allured by the most brilliant, if not the most heroic, form of apostleship. But it was not to be by preaching or by martyrdom that she was to do her share for the triumph of the Faith; it was by prayer and suffering.

It may happen also that we take as an end what in God's thought is only a means. A young priest, fond of literature, thinks about writing dramas or romances. But is he sure that he must use his talent in that way? If he has the gift of style, perhaps he may consecrate it to Christian apologetics. He has to see for himself, but it is not in consulting only his taste that he will know the will of God.

The best way to avoid deception by false calls is to compare the doubtful signals with those that are certain. An order from superiors is obligatory if it conforms to God's law. A civil law is not a law if it is unjust. We may safely follow our inclinations when they lead us to imitate the examples of Christ, and our safety becomes entire when an experienced director approves our steps. Especially when dealing with the spiritual life, it is true to say that we never are too sure. The excess of safety here is better than the defect.

---

[141] St. John of the Cross (1542-1591), mystical Doctor and joint founder of the Discalced Carmelites.

God's Providence Explained

God forbids you to worry about the future

When we know our special vocation and our actual duty, all is well. There is no need to scrutinize the fogs of the future and ask restless questions. I know well that we must not march at random and that fruitful action demands an aim, a plan, and a program. Foresight is a part of prudence.

I know also that God does not forbid a wise economy. Those who insure themselves against accidents, fire, unemployment, and old age are not to be blamed. It is true that some religious institutions make it a law to live day by day, leaving Providence to assist them. It was the principle of St. Teresa never to accept foundations or pensions. She thought herself warranted to do so by that passage of Holy Scriptures in which God commands the Hebrews not to gather an extra supply of manna.[142] But to this text may be opposed others. Indeed, Joseph is praised for having saved the people of Egypt by laying up an abundance of grain for the years of famine.

Foresight is, therefore, lawful, and even necessary. But such foresight must never become a self-torment. Many fidgety people are like that hero of the Greek comedy whose title means the Self-Tormenter.[143] They torture their mind; they spend their time toying with thorns. *If* and *but* are the most frequently used words in their vocabulary. "My God," they groan, "what shall I become if there is another war, if I am sick again, if I lose my money . . . ?"

---

[142] Exod. 16:4, 19.

[143] Terence's *Heauton Timorumenos*, which was adapted from a play of the same name by Menander.

Others, self-confident, see the future quite mirthfully. They are poor today and full of defects, but tomorrow will bring many a surprise; riches and goodness will arrive. Carried away by their imagination, they dream dreams and build castles in Spain, fanciful buildings in which their minds nestle and nod.

We cannot allow ourselves such anticipations. The words of the Master are ever alive: "Be not solicitous for tomorrow; for the morrow will be solicitous for itself. Sufficient for the day is the evil thereof."[144] "And when they shall deliver you up, take no thought how or what to speak. For it is not you that speak, but the Spirit of your Father that speaketh in you."[145] To be harassed with dread and fear is, therefore, to neglect the counsels of the Gospel; it is to insult God's Providence. Since we have a Father in Heaven, why should we weep as though we were orphans?

And common sense agrees with the Gospel. Who knows whether we shall be here tomorrow? Why, then, should we have so much concern with a future that, perhaps, shall never exist?

In one of his parables, Florian speaks of two farmers looking at the clouds. "That means rain," one says, "the good rain so badly needed." "No," says the other, "that is the coming of a hailstorm." They were both wrong. The clouds passed on and brought nothing.

Even if we were sure that our prediction would be realized, it would be stupid to torment ourselves about it. God helps us to bear the pains of today, not of tomorrow. This is why trials

[144] Matt. 6:34.
[145] Matt. 10:19, 20.

seen from afar loom so frightful. They appear bare and stripped of any relief. But when they come, they are wrapped in consolations; and, seeing them so different from what we expected them to be, we say, "Is that all? How foolish was my fear!"

We might imitate the wisdom of that sick child who was asked whether he suffered much. "Yes," he answered, "but the pain of yesterday is gone, and the pain of tomorrow has not yet arrived." Only the present moment is ours. It is needless to add weight to our pains by blending them with remembrance and fears. It is needless also to try to know what our spiritual life will be tomorrow. Shall we acquire such-and-such a virtue? Shall we get rid of a certain vice or bad habit? Idle questions are these. Combined with the attainments of the past, our actual impressions are ceaselessly modified, but none of us can foresee the series of such changes.

Nor need we disturb ourselves concerning the tasks that await us. As though he had foreseen the coming of his death, a young priest wrote this in his notebook: "I will be a day-laborer of God." The day-laborer does not always know what he will do tomorrow. He contents himself with doing day by day, hour by hour, the work for which he is hired. He comes when called and goes when the task is done. Thus, every morning, the Christian takes orders from his Master, and in the evening, he sleeps, happy to have accomplished the work imposed upon him. He is God's day-laborer.

☞

By obedience, you cooperate with Providence

It is not sufficient to enter into the views of God's Providence. As soon as we understand His plans for us, our duty is to set our life in harmony with them.

Earnest, constant, and universal is the docility of a Christian. He yields willingly and immediately to the inspirations of grace; he grasps the least occasions to sanctify himself and edify others. Like the chief of an army who, to hasten the day of victory, mobilizes all the resources of the land, he makes use of all the opportunities that are offered him: a good example, a word heard in passing, a chance meeting, a disappointment, a blow, even a sin. He takes everything to account. Everything helps him to walk one step nearer to God; even obstacles he transforms into means. Although neither punctilious nor captious, he is faithful in little things, for he knows that a trifle may hinder the action of divine grace.

A grain of dust in the movement of a watch is enough to stop it. Still more complex and delicate is the mechanism of the spiritual life. Many remain stationary because they hesitate to offer one little sacrifice. Any other they would offer, but not this; and it is precisely this that God demands.

The call to conversion demands a still more prompt obedience. Jesus, who passes by our way, might not pass again. Imagine a poor wretch who in despair throws himself into a river. He wants to commit suicide, but someone rescues him. He struggles and resists. This is a horrible but true picture of so many sinners who avoid God's help as though they were stubbornly set on their perdition. God pursues them with His entreaties, but on their last refusal of acceptance, He withdraws, and all is over.

Thus, our eternal salvation depends, perhaps, on one word that we are to utter today. One last resistance, itself similar to thousands of others, is tantamount to a moral suicide; it is as though we had pronounced against ourselves a sentence of reprobation. How tragic are some of the most imperceptible acts of the soul!

It is painful at times to obey God. What He commands seems fraught with dangers, and, opposing our own mind to His divine will, we refuse to submit. We think it better to wait for other days before we accept God's orders. Other pretexts come easily. We say, for instance, "I admit that I ought to start my work. But how can I succeed with the resources at hand? It would be imprudent. The Gospel itself advises us to imitate that man who, intending to build a tower, first sits down and reckons the charges that are necessary, and sees whether he have the wherewithal to finish it."[146]

But the Gospel speaks also of shepherds who, on a very vague sign, started out to search for the divine Child.[147] They went, and along their way, other indications were given to them.

It is thus that the great workers wrestle with their task. Before acting, they do not wait to have at hand all the necessary resources. At the first sign, they harness themselves to the task. They follow the star without seeing their path, and as they advance, obstacles fade away.

Others want to be sure of success before acting. They tell you that their labor is not to be wasted, and that if failure cannot be avoided, there is no need to try to prevent it. But the uncertainty of our results is not an excuse for laziness. We have to strive to do our best, but success depends on God. We must do our duty, happen what may.

[146] Cf. Luke 14:28.
[147] Cf. Luke 2:10-15.

⁀

You must accept God's will promptly and joyfully

When, in spite of our diligence, our work comes to nothing, or when we meet with accidents, we have only to bow our head and accept God's will. Yet our resignation must be of the right kind. Some accept the accomplished fact but rebuke God for it. Their submission is sullen, harsh, surly. They yield but reluctantly, and protest against the violence that is offered them. Theirs is the spirit of Stoicism, not of Christianity.

How different is the prompt and joyful resignation of holy souls. Loving God ardently, they unreservedly approve anything that He does. Anything is good that comes from His fatherly hand. In the days of storm and stress, these souls repeat the words of Christ in His agony: "The chalice which my Father hath given me, shall I not drink it?"[148] Whatever be the bitterness of this beverage, it is excellent for them, since their Father has prepared it. Therefore, they take it not only without dislike but with joy. There is so much enthusiasm in their assent that it is hard for them to appear merely resigned.

It is well known how St. Thérèse of Lisieux accepted the seasons' discomforts. How cheerful she was and how charming! Since it is God who allows them, she seemed to say, it would be ungracious on our part to complain. If she happened to rub her hands in winter or to wipe her brow during the hot weather, it was very quickly — on the sly, so that God might not notice it, as she smilingly wrote.

A lovely virtue, then, is resignation. And yet it is usually despised. "A lazy virtue," worldlings call it, "a debasing virtue

[148] John 18:11.

that hinders progress and impairs our dignity. They are cowards who accept evils that they could avoid if they had some courage. It is not in kissing his chains but in breaking them that a man brings honor to himself. Instead of being taught resignation, people ought to be incited against the authors of their misery. Submission and humility are virtues fit for slaves; but for an oppressed citizen, revolt is the most sacred of rights and a most imperious duty."

Ridiculous assertions! Since when are patience and activity incompatible? When have sloth and indolence been entered into the catalog of Christian virtues? It is socialism, not the Gospel, that has spoken of the right to laziness.

☞

Providence calls for action

The Divine Book leads to vigilance and endeavor: "Seek and you shall find; knock and it will be opened unto you."[149] "The kingdom of Heaven suffereth violence, and the violent bear it away."[150] These are the words of Christ.

So, even in the work of our sanctification and salvation, God demands our cooperation. Without Him we can do nothing, but this is no reason to believe that He does all in us. We are living beings whom He has endowed with spontaneity. If He has supplied us with faculties, it is certainly so that we may use them. Our natural resources are, as it were, a little providence to which He invites us to have recourse. He will not let us unload on Him the burdens that we ourselves must bear. Passivity displeases Him as much as resistance. "Open

---

[149] Matt. 7:7.
[150] Matt. 11:12.

thy mouth wide," He tells us through the psalmist, "and I will fill it."[151] When He offers us His grace, the least we can do is accept it.

It is, therefore, a false concept that worldlings have of Christian resignation. Regardless of their charges, it does not exclude activity or initiative. Christians submit themselves to the will of God, but because, in mostly all cases, this will is manifested only by facts, we must act in order to know it.

For instance, suppose you become seriously ill. Does God desire to heal you? You know not, and precisely because of this, you must send for a doctor and follow his prescriptions. The result will tell you of God's decision.

Or say you are engaged in business. You should work — work hard — move Heaven and earth, and if you do not succeed, then, and then only, resign yourselves to the divine will.

God even asks us to contribute to the extension of His kingdom. There are some who think that the welfare of the Church is God's affair more than ours. "God will provide," they say. Evidently God will always defend His interests, but, in doing so, he vouchsafes to accept us as His instruments. It is through the agency of natural causes that He fashions the delicate tissue of flowers, and it is through the ministry of apostles that He purifies and sanctifies human souls. When they go astray, and when faith waxes cold, we must be in a position to say, "It is not through my fault; I have done all that I could for the cause of God."

It is thus that Christians display their activity. If successful, they thank and glorify their divine Coworker; if they fail, they

[151] Ps. 80:11 (RSV = Ps. 81:10).

say with joy, or at least with serenity, "Let it be so, since it is Thy holy will, O God."

☞

Prayer is part of
God's providential design

Not satisfied with having recourse to human means, Christians follow the advice of their Savior to pray without ceasing, to pray and not to faint, and to imitate that widow who, at first rejected by the judge, applied and appealed to him so much that at last he avenged her.[152] Our Lord could have added that we must take Him as our model. He prayed many whole nights, worshiping and thanking His Father for His disciples, and indeed for Himself. In the Garden of Gethsemane, did He not beg His Father to take from Him the burden of suffering, if such was His will?[153]

It may be objected here that, in speaking to God, words are not necessary. Are not our souls translucent to Him? All that we can do is to let Him see our misery as a poor, tattered, and starving Lazarus who in silence presents himself at the door of Dives.[154] The craving for perfection, the groan of an unselfish soul, is tantamount to a continuous prayer. "My God," exclaimed Ernest Hello, "I am before Thee as a brook that is dry, mutely calling for rain." There is eloquence in a silent supplication.

Deists of all schools and stripes have bitterly criticized the prayer of petition. Let it pass that a man places himself in the

---

[152] Cf. Luke 18:1-5.
[153] Matt. 26:39.
[154] Luke 16:19 ff.

presence of God and acknowledges His sovereignty, but why ask Him for health, fortune, and good weather? Can a movement of my heart and my lips change the course of things? God's will is immutable and unalterable, so what He has decided from all eternity must necessarily happen. Besides, He knows our needs better than we do. Is it not more reasonable to rely on Him than to send Him petitions that often are inconsiderate?

It is true that an eternal and immutable will has forever ruled the course of things. But our prayers have been foreseen, as well as have the other facts, and in consideration of these prayers, God has decided to grant us such-and-such a grace. He knows our needs better than we do, and for this very reason, He hears us beyond our desires. We ask for health, and He gives us patience. Instead of the tiny favor that would have satisfied us, He gives us many of them.

But even though we do not always ask Him for what is best, His desire is that we address to Him our requests. Even when mistaken in its object, our prayer at least has this advantage: it reminds us of our condition. God is the only self-sufficient being. Creatures subsist only in Him and by Him, and we acknowledge this fact by prayer. In exposing our needs, we admit the fact of our indigence and dependence; we maintain ourselves in a tendency that agrees with our state — humility and confidence.

Rationalists, therefore, wrongly disparage the prayer of request. Proud of their wisdom, they have left prayer to children and women, simply because they are not truly religious — that is to say, they do not distrust themselves and do not know how to bow before the divine Majesty.

We have seen how simply and easily Christianity blends resignation, activity, and prayer. Its adherents pray as though everything depended on God, and work as though everything depended on their own industry. As deeply as anybody else, they desire to reach their aims; but, before all, they desire that the will of God be fulfilled, and so whatever happens they are always satisfied. When they meet with obstacles that they cannot overcome, they are neither crushed nor disappointed, for they know that their failure contributes to a providential design. God's will is done; this is the source of their joy.

Providence calls for your gratitude

Although our homage adds nothing to His bliss, God is pleased with our thanksgiving. We know by the Gospel how sensitive our Savior was to ingratitude. After having healed ten lepers, He told them to go to Jerusalem and show themselves to the priests. One only, finding he was cured, came back to Him; and he was a Samaritan. Seeing him, Jesus said with sadness, "'Were not all the ten healed? And where are the nine? Were there none to come back and praise God, except this stranger?'"[155]

Imbued with the teaching of the divine Master, the first Christians took to heart never to deserve such rebuke. In the primitive Mass, thanksgiving held a large place; hence the name *Eucharist* ("thanksgiving") given to the Sacrament of the Altar. The voice of Liturgy frequently reminds us of the great duty of gratitude. It invites us to thank God after each Mass, after each canonical hour of the Divine Office, and after

[155] Luke 17:17-18.

each meal. A thought of thanks to God ought frequently be in our heart, since we receive gifts from Him unceasingly.

Unfortunately the very continuity of His gifts makes us forgetful and ungrateful. We are fashioned in such a way that the habitual possession of a treasure prevents us from appreciating its price. To realize it, we have to be deprived of it. It has been well said that what is good is what we have not. What would a blind man not give to recover his sight? What would a paralyzed man not give to be able to walk? A great gift, then, it is that we can see, hear, and go anywhere. The simple exercise of our limbs is a never-ending source of semiconscious satisfactions that blend into a sensation of well-being. These are small joys, if you wish, but they have their price.

Again, life itself is a great gift, for it is the unique occasion of acquiring eternal bliss. Every day brings us new graces; every day invites us to enrich ourselves spiritually and gives us the facility to do so. Verily we ought to say every day, as we do at the dawn of Easter, "This is the day which the Lord hath made; let us rejoice and be glad therein."[156]

And how is it possible not to be moved with admiration and gratitude when considering the incessant action of God within us! The Soul of our soul, He strengthens us, He teaches us, and He encourages us. There is not, and there cannot be, a more intimate, more gracious, or more hearty union than this. Because of it, our interior life, so simple and so commonplace apparently, becomes an abyss of light, peace, and joy. In this sanctuary, whose retreats are unfathomable, is hidden a divine Presence that floods us with brightness.

[156] Ps. 117:24 (RSV = Ps. 118:24).

God's Providence Explained

⁘

You must be thankful even for the blessing of suffering

God be blessed for the joys He gives us, and also for the pains He sends us! The sick man who has been saved by a difficult operation does not fail to compliment his surgeon and manifest his gratitude. This is a duty that men often forget to render to God. They wince under the strokes of sorrow, without seeing the compassionate hand that applies them. Every trial is a remedy prescribed by the Physician of our souls.

Without this energetic treatment, what would become of us? If we had organized our life according to our own way, if we had realized the dreams of our youth, then glory, riches, and enjoyments would have been our lot. But what of all this, which is not eternal? What is all this but perhaps an obstacle to our salvation?

O God, thanks be to Thee for having removed those
hindrances along the road to Heaven. Thanks be to Thee for
the gift of suffering. If we have made progress, be it ever so little,
in spiritual life, has it not been under the spur of sorrow?

⁘

God calls you to share your gifts with others

Is it enough to bless God and thank Him? No, for the best way of proving our gratitude to Him is to share with others the gifts that we have received. God is fatherly to us; we must be fatherly to our brethren. We must let fall on them some drops of the divine water that makes us fruitful and cheerful. "Love is like a river," Lacordaire says. "It descends but never reascends." It never reascends, but along its course, it has fertilized the fields and the meadows; it has at least glorified the source whence it emanates. Children give back to their parents only a tiny part of the tenderness and benefits they have received from them. But someday they, too, will create a home of their own; they will have sons and daughters to whom they will transmit the patrimony of which they are trustees, and thus they will pay their debt, by placing into the hands of others what they have received from their benefactors.

We must act likewise. God does not require that we return to Him what He has given us; He is in no need of it. Not so some of our neighbors. Let us love them as God loves us; let us be obliging, serviceable, and devoted, and we will make God's Providence blessed by them — God's Providence whose servants we are.

Chapter Five

*Trust in Providence
brings peace and joy*

"The kingdom of God is not meat and drink, but justice, and peace, and joy in the Holy Spirit."[157] These words of St. Paul seem to be an echo of the Gospel. "The kingdom of God is within you,"[158] said the divine Master. It does not consist in power or in wealth, but in our perfect conformity to the divine will. God reigns in a soul that has no other ambition than to please Him, and He rewards its faithfulness with the words to the servant in the parable: "Enter into the joy of thy Lord."[159]

Peace and joy are the habitual dispositions of a Christian who trusts in Providence. Having no other rule than God's pleasure, patiently accepting all things that happen, he is the most happy of men. In the midst of the worst trials, he finds in his Faith a safe refuge. He cannot prevent cares and anxieties from disturbing the surface of his soul, but inwardly he always has a peaceful place for retreat and rest.

False security does not bring peace

Peace! We all crave peace, but where shall we find it? Is not the life of man on earth a continuous warfare? We have to

[157] Rom. 14:17.
[158] Luke 17:21.
[159] Matt. 25:21.

struggle against the elements, against hurtful plants and animals, against men, against Satan, and even against the unruly inclinations of our own hearts. To be restful in the midst of such a tumult is as difficult as to stay motionless on a ship shaken by a storm.

Some try to find security in amassing external goods. Gold is their god. They covet and idolize it; they work only for it. When at last they have acquired houses, lands, and stocks, they feel they can breathe freely; they believe themselves safe and secure. A false security is this.

Better informed and more clear-sighted, there are men who turn their eyes toward supernatural powers, but, not being guided by the light of Faith, they deceive themselves. Some believe in fate, a blind and mysterious force by which everything in nature is controlled. They sternly accept its decrees. Such belief has at least the advantage of preventing remorse. Let an accident happen, and you do not have to accuse yourself of imprudence or clumsiness: "It was written" — a pleasant formula that dispenses from examination of conscience and from repentance.

Many a conqueror has believed in his star of destiny. Those great movers of men knew quite well that their success depended only partly upon their efforts. They knew quite well that to stop their triumphal march, a slight incident would be enough, an incident they could not foresee. They strove to tear any weapon from the hands of fate. But not being able to do so, they tried to fancy that they were the favorites of fortune. They imagined that they were born under a lucky star, and when the nights were clear, they glanced with admiration and gratitude on the brilliant star that presided at their destiny.

During the war, when men felt so keenly the need of divine protection, many unbelievers who despised scapulars and medals carried talismans with them. And they still do so today. What a shame for our contemporaries so infatuated with science to lower themselves to such vain and stupid practices! Bossuet was right when he said that when the light of Faith is extinguished, people have to satisfy themselves with the candle end of superstition!

Neither wealth nor superstition can save us from anxiety, but what of philosophy? On the summit of a hill, towering above the restless plain where lives the crowd, is there for us a temple of serenity? Yes, reply the Stoics. Human reason, which is a spark of God's fire, points out the way that leads to interior peace. It teaches us how to discriminate between the things that depend on us, such as wisdom and virtue, and the things over which we have no control, such as health, reputation, and riches. According to the Stoics, the things that do not depend on us are not for our good. They have no value to those who are truly wise. Throughout the vicissitudes of life a Stoic must remain calm and unmoved. Pain to him is merely a word. He is the man without a tear.

Stoicism, then, is based on an error and a contradiction. It is true that virtue is above health. But to deny that health is a valuable gift is to go against all evidence. Stoics looked upon virtue and wisdom as essentials. Very well, but to be wise and virtuous, the first condition is to be alive, and, to remain alive, we have to be clothed, fed, and financed.

If the end is desirable, why not the means? Yes, but if you desire them, if you run after things that do not depend on you, how can you help becoming restless? You are at the mercy of sheer emergency; you are carried away like flotsam and jetsam on a stormy sea. Stoics, therefore, were compelled either to be anxious like other people, or to close their eyes to evidence. It is this latter plan that they adopted. But the mind cannot for long be fed on illusions; we can rest in truth alone. Stoicism is dead: it is a doctrine that no one can accept.

⌒

God's Providence brings peace

Well known is St. Teresa's bookmark : "Let nothing disturb you, nothing frighten you." A strange motto for a nun! You wonder why this great Carmelite borrows from the Stoics their famous maxim: *nil mirari* ("to look upon nothing"). But straightway she adds this:

> All things are passing;
> God never changes;
> Patient endurance
> Attains to all things;
> In him who possesses God
> Nothing is wanting:
> God alone suffices.

It is not in herself, then, it is not in the light of her reason, it is not in the strength of her will that she seeks a support and a stay; to God Himself, to God alone she wends her way to find her Helper.

The psalmist of old acts likewise. To him the Lord is a "rock" and a "refuge."[160] The Eternal watches over him as we do over the apple of our eye; it is under His guardianship that

[160] Ps. 70:3 (RSV = Ps. 71:3).

he nestles in peace, as baby birds under the shelter of their mother's wings. Here are snatches of his songs: "I laid me down and slept; I awaked, for Jehovah sustaineth me."[161] "He delivers the needy when he crieth, and the poor that hath no helper."[162] "Oh, how great is Thy goodness which Thou hast laid up for them that fear Thee."[163]

Such security as the Jews expected from the Eternal, Jesus had pledged and promised to His disciples — a proof, by the way, that He was aware of His Godhead. "Take up my yoke upon you and learn of me, because I am meek and humble of heart, and you will find rest to your souls."[164]

He holds in His hand the golden key that opens the City of Peace. Isaiah, seeing Him along the vistas of the future, greeted Him as "the Prince of Peace."[165] When this Prince was born in Bethlehem, His gift of joyful advent was peace — peace on earth to men of good will.[166] And when He departed from this world, what did He bequeath us? Peace — His own peace. "Peace I leave with you: my peace I give unto you; not as the world giveth do I give unto you. Let not your heart be troubled, nor let it be afraid."[167]

There are some people who, lacking confidence in God, and thinking of their errors and faults, continually reproach

---

[161] Cf. Ps. 3:6 (RSV = Ps. 3:5).

[162] Cf. Ps. 71:12 (RSV = Ps. 72:12).

[163] Cf. Ps. 30:20 (RSV = Ps. 31:19).

[164] Matt. 11:29.

[165] Isa. 9:6.

[166] Luke 2:14.

[167] John 14:27.

themselves: "Fool that I was! I could have been so good, so great, so well loved by God and by men. But through my cowardice and stupidity, I have endangered and lost everything. It is too late now to rebuild my life. Woe is me! I have missed my destiny!"

There is nothing so bitter as this sensation of irreparableness. But to one who believes in the heavenly Father, life is not and can never be a bankruptcy. "A man is never an entire failure unless and until he goes to Hell." His failings have been permitted for his sanctification. If they have rendered him more humble, more resigned, or more pious, he cannot complain. They have been a gain rather than a loss, and it may be said that such defeats are as glorious as victories.

☞

Confidence in God brings
you peace of conscience

Confidence in God also shelters us from scrupulosity, that moral disease which is so hurtful and so hard to cure. To spend your time in sifting, scrutinizing, and searching your conscience, to believe yourself guilty always and everywhere, to see enormous sins in the least peccadillo, to count and recount the sins of your life, and to declare them again and again until you have exhausted the patience of any confessor — this merely supposes much attachment to your own opinion, much obstinacy, and much egoism. Scruples are a form of fear.

But when one sincerely loves God, one thinks of Him much more than of self. A true lover of God does not injure His name by thinking that He is stern, inexorable, and pitiless, when, as a matter of fact, He commands us ever to forgive from the bottom of our heart, not only once, and not only seven

times, but seventy times seven times[168] — that is to say, indefinitely. A true lover of God does not doubt the word of His
ministers, who have said in His name, "I absolve thee of thy
sins." Instead of thinking of the past whose indebtedness has
been liquidated by absolution, he strives to repair it by a more
fervent life, following in this the example of a famous writer
who said, "I correct my books in writing better ones."

Is not this filial confidence more agreeable to God than the
continual terror of a soul consumed by scruples? Do you think
that our heavenly Father enjoys to see us trembling before
Him? Is He more honored by fear than by love? No one who
has read the Gospels can believe this.

⌒

Faith in Providence preserves you
from perplexity, agitation, and dread

Like the legendary Sphinx, life lays down problems that
must be solved immediately and sometimes under pain of
perdition. Sickness comes, and recovery perhaps depends on
the doctor to be chosen. For whom shall we send? If we post-
pone our decision, the illness will grow worse. If our choice is
bad, we have less chance to get better. So are the perplexities
of those who imagine that everything depends on their own
calculations and foresight.

But a true Christian knows that he is not alone in direct-
ing his life. God, whom he invokes, presides over his delibera-
tions; and if his only aim is to please God, he has no regret to
entertain, whatever decision he takes. His faith, of course,
does not dispense him from labor, but when he has done his

---

[168] Matt. 18:21.

best, he is at peace; very different from those restless persons whose activity ever degenerates into fever. There is no pain like this consciousness of responsibility. If I feel convinced that the solution of a difficulty depends merely on me, farewell to my joy and my peace! I have to watch and wrestle night and day. Not a moment of intermission before success or exhaustion.

Whence comes this feverish agitation? It comes of the fact that the divine Master's advice has been ignored: "Seek ye first the kingdom of God and His justice, and all these things shall be added unto you."[169] It is "all these things" that are first desired. The intention is not right; there is disorder, and disorder ever breeds uneasiness and anxiety. If my only desire were to please God, mine would be a life of happiness. Not that activity would die within me; I would work according to God's order, but without excess and disturbance.

God never asks anything impossible. He is pleased with the peaceful and regular movement of a soul less attentive to its task than to His good pleasure. He withdraws from that overbusy crowd of men who never think they have done enough until they have reached their goal.

A true Christian is indifferent to success, or, rather, he is always sure of success, for to him success consists in pleasing God. "He that shall persevere to the end," whom the hour of death shall find still struggling to gain the height, although perhaps beginning at the base for the thousandth time, "shall be saved,"[170] and God, in one purgatorial pang, will perfect the

[169] Matt. 6:33.
[170] Cf. Matt. 10:22.

unfinished task and will bring the storm-tossed, weary soul "to the haven of its desire."

And why should we be afraid of what the future has in store for us? Will God leave us in need if we work for Him? He has given us His only Son; will He refuse to give us our daily bread? Will He send us trials without sending also the strength to bear them? Well, then, let us have confidence in Him, knowing that, if He should plunge us into the abyss, even then He will be with us.

⟨⁓⟩

Peace can coexist with suffering

Does this mean that, thus ensconced in the stronghold of God's will, a Christian is safe from all adversity? No, for here below, there is no perfect security. The peace we taste is mixed with alarms, pains, and uneasiness, and rightly so. It is to be remembered that Christ has not promised happiness, but peace, to His disciples. Happiness supposes exemption from all pains, and satisfaction of all desires.

Now, when we think of the number of instinctive and appetitive tendencies that psychologists call sensitiveness, when we know that each fiber of our body may be the seat of a suffering, we see immediately why happiness is not of this world. It is composed of so many elements that there is always one missing. How can we satisfy at the same time contrary inclinations? What the flesh craves, the spirit holds in horror, and vice versa. Whatever design you take, you always displease someone.

Absolute happiness will always be lacking here, but we may acquire interior peace. Such peace, such orderly peace, which Jesus had promised, results from the perfect harmony between our will and His own. The ever-present consciousness of His nature is a happiness that can coexist with suffering. "I exceedingly abound with joy in all our tribulations,"[171] we may then say with St. Paul.

How can this be done? How can the soul which is simple take at the same time two contrary attitudes? It is a mystery that I cannot explain, but it is a fact attested by numberless testimonies and by our own personal experience. "The saints lead joyous lives even amidst their austerities and sufferings," says Father Faber. "Blind as we are, we can see that there is a vaster joy in one hour of a saint's holiness than in all the outspread mediocrity of lives like ours, prolonged for any number of years. If all emanations of God are joyous, holiness is confessedly the most joyous of them all. Have we ourselves ever experienced a joy in life which was equal to the common joy of being in a state of grace? But the joy of holiness is this joy intensified, and perhaps indeed it is something more than even that. Holiness is a very spacious thing, and God always fills in all hearts all the room which is left Him there. But holiness is not only an exceeding joy, but it is gifted with a serene capacity of enjoying its own joy, which is by no means universal in the case of other joys."

Interior peace can coexist also with legitimate apprehensions. Despite his complete submission to the divine will, St. Paul was harassed by the care of souls and by his "solicitude for all the churches." "Who is weak and I am not weak?" he said to the Corinthians. "Who is scandalized and I am not on fire?"[172]

[171] 2 Cor. 7:4.
[172] 2 Cor. 11:28-29.

When a mother thinks of the dangers that threaten the life, the perseverance, and the eternal salvation of her child — when, over the cradle where he sleeps, she sees the coming cross — how could she not be alarmed? Her own sorrows she heartily accepts, but has she the right to resign herself to the sufferings of those she loves?

⌒

Trust in God's Providence will perfect you

Here, again, it is in conformity to the divine will that consolation is found. When we have done all we can to soothe, edify, and save our brethren, we must leave the rest in God's hands. He will provide and supply better than we can. Nothing will happen that He has not wisely and justly ordained. We must bow before His blessed will in complete submission.

Such complete and constant submission leads to perfection. It first supposes a very lively faith. There is no Christian who denies God's Providence, but there is many a step from belief to practice. All men know that God is present everywhere, and yet many live as though they were alone. They are weak, sad, and discouraged. They have not the spirit of faith. God is near them and offers them His help, and His help is ignored and spurned.

Trust in God's Providence also demands that we detach ourselves from creatures. We follow the impulse of grace only when we are detached from all earthly ties. Then only can we say with sincerity, "My God, I am Your servant. Let it be done to me according to Your word. I will what You will — nothing less, nothing more."

Such detachment must go as far as indifference, holy indifference. Passive acceptance is not enough. Some are poor, but they wish to be rich. To a soul that trusts in God, the things that matter are not plenty or poverty, health or illness. One thing only is worthwhile: God's good pleasure in the soul. The soul cannot, of course, be indifferent to its spiritual progress, but it desires it in the very measure willed by God. The soul stands on its guard against self-love, which slips in everywhere, even in the conquest of humility.

We wish to have nothing to be reproached for; we wish to give to our soul the harmony, the brightness, the purity, and the grace of a flower. Why? To please God, no doubt; but also in order that we may be proud of victory and taste the joys of triumph. There is in this a self-love, a subtle egotism contrary to the self-denial mentioned in the Gospel. To keep up from such vain complacency, God leaves us in a state of imperfection. He lets us live with our defects, as with troublesome guests, incessantly reminding us of our misery and weakness. Fight them we must; strive to rid ourselves of them we must; but gently, not bitterly. We must be patient with ourselves, since God is patient with us.

Must this holy indifference go so far as a loss of interest in our salvation? Quietists went so far as to reply in the affirmative. "Lord," they said, "save me or damn me. I shall be happy, even in Hell, if such is Your will." Such extravagance may seem heroic, but how false and dangerous it is! How can we love God if we have not the desire to see Him and possess Him? How can we believe that the heavenly Father takes pleasure in torturing His children merely to test their fidelity? So inconstant and feeble, could our soul patiently endure endless punishments? As ardent as we may suppose it, can charity be sufficient to sustain our soul's courage during a whole eternity? No!

Let us not, therefore, dream such dreams. Let us desire the eternal bliss that God desires for us.

And yet we must do so in thinking more of Him than of ourselves. Living for Him, we may leave in His hands the care of our salvation. There will be no loss on our part if we do this, and in fact we will gain much. For we are dealing with a Master who is infinitely rich and never lets Himself be outdone in generosity. If we work for Him, He will work for us. He will refuse nothing to those who refuse nothing to Him. But great love is needed to surrender ourselves in such a manner without any reservation.

There are also degrees of piety. Some make their religion subservient to their interests and aim merely at consolation and support. Others, fired by a great zeal for the glory of God, spend themselves completely for the extension of His reign. For all that, they do not forget themselves and are led to labor by the hope of a magnificent reward.

Others, again, serve God without any thought of self. They are engulfed in Him. They are only docile instruments. Having no will of their own, they deliver themselves to the genius of divine grace. God can ask them anything and mold them according to His wish.

A person so surrendered thinks no more of the past nor of the future. Having confessed, regretted, and expiated his faults, he hopes that God will not be severe with him and blindly throws himself into the abyss of His mercy. He lets God lead him according to His will, without asking how long he will remain in this world or how his plans will end. He lives in the present, applying himself to his task. To fulfill the duty of the present hour is his only desire.

God's Providence Explained

~

Peace comes to those who do God's will

Those who do God's will day by day, hour by hour, are like the hand of a clock that points out the seconds one after another and which, although constantly moving, is always in its right place. They have the sensation of well-being, of contributing their share to the march of the universe, and of being a well-regulated part in that immense mechanism. It is to the soul a real sweetness, a joy wholly spiritual, but pure and profound and destined to last forever.

Now, do not believe that, because confined in the present, our life becomes narrow and poor. On the contrary, we then discover vaster horizons than those merely touching an earthly future. What is our present duty but an order from God? To conform ourselves to it in a spirit of faith is to commune with the infinite. As Jean Pierre de Caussade says, "God's will is an abyss whose opening is the present moment; plunge into that abyss, and you will find it infinitely larger than your desires."

Fidelity to the duty of the present moment augments also our grace and glory. What is one hour spent in God's service? Seemingly nothing; it passes so quickly. And yet such hours contain eternity. Every moment of our life, every heartbeat, every spark of thought has for us eternal consequences. Oh, the grandeur, the beauty, of Christian life! The boundless and radiant vistas it opens to us every moment!

And the serenity it gives us! A soul that has surrendered to God is established in peace. It tastes the blissful peace that surpasses all understanding. Nothing can astonish it; nothing can disconcert it. In love with God's will, the soul is satisfied with anything that happens. It meets with no obstacle, no mishap, no storm. All is well, for all contributes to the soul's personal sanctification and to the designs of God.

On the contrary, those who hanker after temporal goods are at the mercy of the winds. Let an accident occur, an epidemic, a tempest, and all their plans fall to the ground. They pass from hope to fear according to the tidings each day brings them. Standing on the surface of a sphere that turns on itself, they follow all its motions and are sometimes crushed by it.

But those who live in God and for God, having taken shelter in the center of all things, remain motionless while around them everything is storm-tossed.

$\backsim$

God watches over you with fatherly care

Although He has not promised happiness in this present life, Jesus asks His disciples to rejoice, even in the midst of trials: "Blessed are ye when they shall revile you, and persecute you, and speak all that is evil against you, untruly, for my sake. Be glad and rejoice, for your reward is very great in Heaven."[173]

Here, again, the powerful voice of St. Paul echoes the Gospel: "Rejoice in the Lord always," he says to the Philippians. "Again I say, rejoice. The Lord is nigh."[174] Yes, the Lord is near us — so near is He that He dwells and acts in us by His grace. He protects and loves us. He directs our individual life and the march of humanity. He tells us that the world is not a chaos, a mass of atoms hurled into an empty infinitude. It is His masterpiece, which He has created for His glory, a poem of which each of us is a conscious and imperishable stanza. Yes, indeed,

[173] Matt. 5:11-12.
[174] Phil. 4:4.

life is worth living, and the endless career that it opens for us hereafter allows us to nurture great hopes and entertain vast thoughts.

An unbeliever once said to me, "Oh, the happy days when as a small child I could think only of Father, Mother, and God!" Yes, the happy days of childhood! How good it is to nestle in caressing arms, feeling sure that we are taken care of so much better than we could care for ourselves. A child has an unlimited confidence in his parents, upon whom he looks as semidivine protectors. He invokes also the heavenly Father when his is a Christian home. From such security of his tender years, he derives a constant need of kindness and protection. Therefore, what a sorrow is his when he loses his parents! Even in middle age, he feels his orphaned state.

And what a rending of heart if, through his fault, his religious beliefs die within him. The world, without God and the prospect of another life, appears to him narrow and dark like the vault of a jail. He is despondent like an exile on his way toward his country who suddenly hears that his birthplace has disappeared in a cataclysm — no one henceforth to think of him, no one to help him. He is alone to struggle against the forces allied against him.

But a Christian who trusts in God as his heavenly Father is like those well-provided sons who know nothing of fear; theirs is the song of the poet:

> Fear not, my soul, the coming years:
> God into pearls shall turn your tears.
> Be like the bird who ever sings
> Because he knows that he has wings.

Life is that frail branch that leans because of our weight and that is shaken by the wind. No anxiety, however; let us be peaceful and joyful, for we have wings — faith and hope — that will not only prevent us from falling down, but will carry us to the heights.

There are conscientious guardians who fulfill their task dutifully and decently, but without alacrity and cordiality. But it is not so with God's Providence, which watches over us in a fatherly manner. To be loved by God, boundlessly so, prodigally so — what a consolation there is in such thought!

✑

Providence shows that life has a magnificent meaning

When we consider the tiny place we occupy in the universe, we are sometimes tempted to despise ourselves. Puny, insignificant beings that we are, our absence could not be noticed. But let us not absolutely disregard human nature. It is true that we are miserable — more than miserable, because of our littleness and our sins. But in a certain way, we are very great. We are only "a little less than the angels,"[175] says the psalmist. And what makes us great is not only that we are able to think, but that we are loved by God. In spite of our native corruption, our vileness, and our numberless sins, there must be within us something rare and excellent, since the Almighty vouchsafes to look upon us and to protect us with so much solicitude.

It is a joy to know that life has a meaning, a magnificent meaning. What is it to those who do not believe in God's Providence? A drudgery or a pleasure party. Some work to eat,

[175] Ps. 8:6 (RSV = Ps. 8:5); Heb. 2:7.

eat to live, and live without knowing why. Others think only about pleasure and what they call a "good time."

But what signifies this restless and aimless labor, as vain as the perpetual motion of the sea waves? What can we think of that ghastly festivity which usually ends in ghastly death?

If life is only an *ignis fatuus*, a little flame that flickers for a moment on the surface of the earth and then goes out, it is right to despise it. And no wonder so many unbelievers sink so easily into pessimism. To such unhappy men who have no hope, life is a tiny thing ending in nothingness. Life to them is a blind alley, abruptly abutting upon the black wall of death. It is impossible to retrace their steps. Sooner or later they are crushed on that wall, and they fall into dust.

On the other hand, Christian faith leads to optimism. The English poet Algernon Swinburne and his cohort may taunt Christianity as having darkened human existence by projecting upon it the sinister shadow of Hell. Happy the pagans who could satisfy their passions without any thought of the hereafter! Following their example, let us banish every superstitious fear. Since there will be no account, let our instincts be free in the house of mirth.

This is easily said, but before accepting such advice, we must do away with poverty, hard labor, illness, old age, and death. It is sheer mockery to preach this doctrine of pleasure to a laborer who toils from early morning until night or to a mother sorrowing over the loss of her only son. To enjoy any amusement, it is necessary to be in high spirits, to have health, and to have money. How few have all that! Look on those around you: see how many have their heart wounded, their aspirations thwarted, and their lives disappointed. Most men drag to the grave the heavy chain of their baffled hopes. It is true that death is to them a deliverance; but if this is their only consolation, they will find it, I think, rather insufficient. What joy will they have left to them when they have lost the reason for life, and when they can look for nothing beyond the tomb? They have shaken off all illusions, and all the world to them is bitter as a tear.

Christians, on the other hand, know nothing of such disenchantment. Life, be it ever so humble, is interesting to them. They look upon it as a workshop where the divine Sculptor fashions us according to the likeness of His Son. He prepares here below the recruits of the heavenly Jerusalem, the City Splendid, where, in the splendors of divine light, the elect will be happy forever. Oh, the happy perspective! How not to wait with expectation like the psalmist of old who, when he was marching toward Sion, cried out with joyous enthusiasm, "I was glad at the things that were said unto me: We will go into the house of the Lord!"[176]

⌒

Faith in Providence will bring you
happiness, here and hereafter

Thus it is that Christian hope projects on all things a reflection that transfigures them. Seen in that light, the world no more appears as an undecipherable enigma. Scientists notice only the details — so much so, that they lose sight of the whole. By dint of patience and industry, they snatch from nature some of its secrets, but they never reach its physical questions with which they cannot deal.

[176] Ps. 121:1 (RSV = Ps. 122:1).

God's Providence Explained

The few philosophers who are busy with such problems never arrive at any agreement. Instead of enlightening us, they merely heap up clouds. Faith alone teaches what human reason is powerless to discover. Undoubtedly it does not answer the thousand and one questions asked by our insatiable curiosity. But it actually does more than this: it gives us a full view of the whole universe. With Faith as a guide, diversity is reduced into unity. History, which at first blush is only a jumble of events, is set in good order and harmony. Everything is simplified and embellished. The marvelous power of Christian chemistry transmutes sadness into joy, disorder into harmony, and ugliness into beauty!

Faith in God's Providence has the further advantage of enlarging the mind and making it conceive several kinds of beauty. There are people who enjoy only a certain kind of scenery; for instance, the geometrical precision of a Dutch garden. Others admire all the aspects of nature, even the freedom of some pathless wilderness. So it is with those who strive to have all events turn according to their desires. They enjoy life only if it is conformed to their aspirations and fashioned according to their whims. They are dreamers who at any moment hide themselves in the Spanish castles built by their fancy. They like to dwell where they cannot dwell and have what they cannot have. Theirs is the worst condition of all.

Others, more adaptable, adjust themselves to the events that come. They cheerfully accept everything that arrives along their way, for everything that arrives carries a divine mark. Always satisfied with their destiny, they sing a hymn of thanksgiving even in the midst of the worst trials. They are happy.

Sophia Institute Press®

Sophia Institute is a nonprofit institution that seeks to restore man's knowledge of eternal truth, including man's knowledge of his own nature, his relation to other persons, and his relation to God. Sophia Institute Press® serves this end in numerous ways: it publishes translations of foreign works to make them accessible for the first time to English-speaking readers; it brings back into print books that have long been out of print; and it publishes important new books that fulfill the ideals of Sophia Institute. These books afford readers a rich source of the enduring wisdom of mankind.

Sophia Institute Press® makes these high-quality books available to the general public by using advanced technology and by soliciting donations to subsidize its general publishing costs. Your generosity can help Sophia Institute Press® to provide the public with editions of works containing the enduring wisdom of the ages. Please send your tax-deductible contribution to the address below. We also welcome your questions, comments, and suggestions.

For your free catalog, call:
Toll-free: 1-800-888-9344

or write:
Sophia Institute Press® ◆ Box 5284 ◆ Manchester, NH ◆ 03108

or visit our website:
www.sophiainstitute.com

Sophia Institute is a tax-exempt institution as defined by the Internal Revenue Code, Section 501(c)(3). Tax I.D. 22-2548708.